Soul Murmurs

Seasonal words of spiritual
wisdom to enlighten the soul

Anita Neilson

BOOKS
Winchester, UK
Washington, USA

JOHN HUNT PUBLISHING

First published by O-Books, 2019
O-Books is an imprint of John Hunt Publishing Ltd., 3 East St., Alresford,
Hampshire SO24 9EE, UK
office@jhpbooks.net
www.johnhuntpublishing.com
www.o-books.com

For distributor details and how to order please visit the 'Ordering' section on our website.

Text copyright: Anita Neilson 2018

ISBN: 978-1-78904-111-8
978-1-78904-112-5 (ebook)
Library of Congress Control Number: 2018941007

A CIP catalogue record for this book is available from the British Library.

Design: Cecilia Perriard

UK: Printed and bound by CPI Group (UK) Ltd, Croydon, CR0 4YY
US: Printed and bound by Thomson-Shore, 7300 West Joy Road, Dexter, MI 48130

**We operate a distinctive and ethical publishing philosophy in
all areas of our business, from our global network of authors to
production and worldwide distribution.**

Contents

Summer

Autumn

Winter

Other Books by the Author

Acts of Kindness from Your Armchair, Ayni Books 2017.
ISBN: 978-1-78535-617-9
An exploration of how we can make a meaningful
contribution to the world through simple acts of kindness,
all easily done from home. The book acts as a practical
guide to the ways in which thoughts, words and acts
of kindness, both inward and towards the wider world,
can create real change.

Goddess When She Rules, Golden Dragonfly Press 2017.
ISBN: 9780998976655
Contributing Author in this extraordinary collection
of poetry and prose penned by spiritual women across
the globe in an exploration of what the Goddess energy
signifies to them.

Preface

Words have the power to heal the greatest hurts, the deepest pains, the longest nights when darkness prevails in the very center of our being. Words convey our feelings, ever-changing with each day. They can be used as a weapon, tipped with the venom of rage and hate, or they can pour over others like a salve, sealing and protecting, gently and warmly conveying our thoughts and emotions. This book centers around the following themes in the main: finding the Divine in the natural world; the power of kindness and compassion to oneself and others; the nature of Divine love; and blissful union with Source through meditation.

This collection of Soul Murmurs—poetry, prayer, affirmation, story and comment—engages the reader on a journey to strip away the outer vestiges of this body-mind which we inhabit: our desires, the ego, gender, race, profession, personality, in order to facilitate reconnection with the soul, our true inner being. We can all transform our lives with the healing power of positive, loving thoughts and words. This book will be your guide along the way. You are sure to find within these pages:

- *Inspiration for living a more spiritual life*
- *Assistance in reevaluating your priorities*
- *Diversion from worries and pain*
- *Guidance on finding the Divine in everyone and everything.*

Some of you may be familiar with my blog *Healing Words: Inspirational Bytes of Calm* from which this book takes its inspiration. The *Healing Words* blog and this book share the same aims which are to teach others how they can contribute to the world simply by a change in outlook; by accessing their inner compassion and love; and by putting these attributes into practice in their daily lives. I hope this collection helps to ignite the flame of transformation within you so that you reestablish a loving relationship with your true Self and see the eternal flame which lies at its heart. In so doing, many of you may also rediscover your love for the Creator.

This book follows on from my first book, *Acts of Kindness from Your Armchair*, which is a practical and spiritual toolkit of ideas and suggestions on how to imbue your life with more kindness, and how to nurture these small acts of kindness in your daily life—regardless of any limitations you may have. These small acts of kindness can and do make a huge difference to the world around us and are all easily done from home.

My writings in general, and specifically the poems contained in this book, are also a reflection of my deeply personal physical, emotional and, most importantly, spiritual journey. As it is for many of us, a time of crisis brought me to my knees physically, mentally and emotionally. I had been a busy, stressed high school teacher, a perfectionist personality, always in competition with others, wanting to be the best, with no time for making friends. I was financially secure and lived a "full" life socializing with colleagues and family and taking many holidays every year. But I was also stressed, agitated, angry, and far too dependent on that large glass of wine or two every evening to try and de-stress. And the realization slowly dawned that there was a sadness at my core, such a longing for something I knew not what. This longing or *spiritual malaise* was accompanied by many physical and emotional symptoms (such as strange twitches; dizziness; loss of energy and *"joie de vivre"*; lack of spatial awareness; persistent pains in various parts of the body; low mood; tearfulness and depression) all of which I stubbornly ignored.

One day though, I was stopped in my tracks by pain and fatigue, rendered completely unable to function at all in normal life. To describe this fatigue is difficult, because we all get fatigue, don't we? But imagine sitting on a comfortable sofa, leaning your head back and feeling as if not only were you sinking into the sofa but that you were being sucked into it, unable to free yourself; then feeling as if a large very heavy rug or carpet were being placed over your body and you were unable to move for an hour or so. This is what overwhelming fatigue felt like to me. It was frightening, and because I had no idea what was wrong with me at the time, I wondered if I would be permanently paralyzed with it. Eventually I learned to ride the storm, knowing that the fatigue would pass after an hour and I would be able to get up and move around again.

The next few years saw me virtually housebound with what were eventually diagnosed as Fibromyalgia, M.E. (Chronic Fatigue Syndrome), depression and anxiety. Little by little a huge number of my capabilities was withdrawn from me: I could no longer walk my dogs, bake cakes, do housework, go out for meals or take trips to the theatre. Being housebound was like falling down a deep well and I was there for a long time. This well was one from which I was even loath to emerge. There's a well-known saying, "Better the devil you know", and I guess I was afraid of what reality held for me on the surface. Yet emerge I did, slowly. I haven't overcome these health issues and I feel intuitively that I won't, but all my efforts seem to have stopped them in their tracks. Now I can say that I have gone from being "housebound" to "home-free". I still spend the majority of my time at home, but my attitude has changed, and this has been the major factor in accepting my new life and enabling it to flourish. If you find yourself in a black hole (or deep well) for whatever reason, I hope this book will help you, I really do. Take it from me, things can and do get better, but we need to work at it!

For me, looking back through the lens of retrospection provides such amazing clarity as to the spiritual malaise underpinning all the physical, mental and emotional symptoms of disease. I was "living the dream" yet unhappiness resided at the core and ill-health was knocking at the door! With the help of friends and family and a few self-help books, I gradually pulled myself out of the well where depression, fatigue and pain were all I focused on, to start my life anew with positivity, gratitude and kindness at the reins. And I began to write, firstly in a journal, then on a blog. I also began to meditate, and in those moments of mindfulness and stillness, I found peace. Lots of peace. That peace brings healing and purpose. And with more peace comes joy and a deep desire to help others find a similar state of peace within themselves. That's why I wrote this book.

Writing can be viewed simply as a creative activity, but if you are willing to surrender to its spiritual essence, it then becomes a means of connecting with your higher Self and with the universal source of knowledge which surrounds us. I would never have believed this in years gone by, but having experienced it for myself, I know it to be true. Poetry and prose started coming through into my mind when I began meditating around 4 years ago. Finding that inner space of quiet, of deep stillness, allows us to disconnect the logical, reasoning mind with all its thoughts and emotions, likes and dislikes and so on, and permits us space, time and opportunity to connect with our true Self, our soul. It is this connection I believe which facilitates my writing and I am so grateful for it. I call it "being in the flow" because words just flow like silk from an unending fountain. And I realize now *why* I possess the skills I was born with and have acquired through this lifetime. Here are some examples. I learned to touch type in school; I learned how to write essays in university; I practiced writing short stories in early adulthood; I learned how to put a point across in an accessible way when I was a teacher; I learned resilience and determination in all areas of my life, thanks to the support of my parents but also a healthy mix of competition with my siblings. All these skills have stood me in good stead for this part of my life. When I look back on childhood and early adulthood, I see it now for what it was—a preparation ground for finding and carrying out my life purpose—to help others through my writing. It is so wonderful to finally find your purpose; to find the answers to the big questions in life: Why are we here? Who am I? Is there a God? and so on.

What sort of writings will you find in *Soul Murmurs*? Its first tentative steps brim over with light poems of the sensory beauty of the external world of Spring: delicate reflections of the awakening or rebirth of the Self. These poems are at times naïve and childlike to announce the young, newly awakened child of God that I was at the beginning of writing this book. Summer heat infuses the soul's journey with a warmth and maturity, of finding oneself in the world, yet somehow observing it, detached—in awe. Autumn's glory is a full-rounded harvest of poems on inner growth, yet ever looking forwards to the cycle of death and renaissance; it is the burning away of earthly connections; a harmonization of our interconnectedness. I think Autumn is my favorite season of all! We finish the passage of the seasons with Winter, a time of deep introspection and stripping away of artifice. Like the trees which shed their leaves to reveal their true structure beneath, so it is with us. When we strip away the masks that we wear, we are left with our true form. This can be vulnerable and empowering in equal measure. The final poem of Winter is a reprise of the first poem of Spring yet infused with an increased wisdom and a clearer understanding of the nature of reality, so that one could begin again at Spring rereading the poems with a greater depth and clarity.

The book's structure is not coincidental, since the passage of the seasons is the passage of all life on Earth. It is an eternal cycle of birth, preservation, dissolution and rebirth. You will notice that through the seasons, the poems develop from finding the Divine in the external world through the senses, to an inner perception of Divinity within ourselves, a turning inwards of the senses to find the glories therein. This journey from exoteric to esoteric echoes the spiritual journey of anyone longing to become closer to God. We begin with outer displays of faith: following dogma, rituals, do's and don'ts, attending church services and so on, but then for the serious seeker the journey turns inward, toward establishing a more personal inner relationship with God, whatever form S/He takes for us. I believe we do this chiefly through meditation when we learn that connecting with our inner stillness *is* connecting with the Creator.

The poems are interspersed with other forms of prose throughout the book: essay, affirmations, articles, short story. The aim is the same—to provide the reader with bytes of calm in a busy day. So, take some time each day to read a page or two. Let its quiet wisdom sit with you as you go about your day and allow your mind and heart to process what it means to and for you. There are some spiritual terms used in the book with which you may not be familiar. In this case, please refer to the Glossary at the back of the book for a brief explanation.

On a technical note, some of the poems are also available to listen to (Audio poems) and to watch (Video poems). In the e-book version, there will be a direct URL clickable link to guide you to the Audio or Video file. In the paperback version, please refer to the Glossary under Audio poems or Video poems for the URL link. Please also note, American spelling has been used throughout.

Anita Neilson

Acknowledgements

Many thanks to Ken Eaton at Natureworks
for his cover artwork: Lone Tree.

Thanks also go to John Hunt Publishing/O-Books
for the professional service they provide to enable spiritual
books to reach the wider world.

This book is dedicated to all those seeking spiritual
advancement. May your journey be a joyous one!

Spring

Introduction to Spring:

I love spring. There's an urgency to everything. Bulbs send up tentative shoots skyward in response to increasing light and warmth. New life is being born everywhere we look. Whose heart hasn't given even a tiny leap at the sight of a lamb jumping around in a field, filled with the simple joy of being alive? It reminds us to slow down and live in the moment, to really enjoy the life we are living. Trees and shrubs begin producing new shoots at this time of year, slowly emerging from their voluntary stasis of winter. Frozen waters crack and groan as the sun's energy stimulates the process of defrosting and metamorphosis from solid to liquid. All life is shedding its protective mask of winter to reveal the hidden life beneath just waiting to burst through and begin again the cycle of rebirth and growth.

Spring usually beckons around March or April in the Northern Hemisphere where I live. Our ancestors knew how important all the seasons were to their survival, and throughout the ages, they sought to personify and glorify the natural world (in this case spring). They believed that by worshipping their gods of fertility in this way, they would be guaranteed a prosperous year ahead with many newborn livestock and a plentiful harvest later. One such example is Persephone. In Ancient Greek mythology, she was the Goddess of spring, but she was also Queen of the Underworld where she reputedly spent her winters before emerging each spring to preside over the beginning of another cycle of life. She must have seemed an all-powerful deity, returning underground after the harvest, unseen until spring came around again. She was the perfect personification of the vernal natural world in action.

Daylight gradually lengthens from midwinter onwards until in spring we reach the equalizing of day and night (equinox).

For me, it's like basking in the drowsy contentment of awakening from a deep sleep, emerging into the dazzling display of blue skies and spring flowers, such as daffodils, iris and bluebells. The opening of the cherry blossom, Japan's national flower, signals the onset of spring there and cherry blossom festivals are held all over the country in the spring months. These are called *Hanami* ("viewing flowers") and families and communities meet in parks and gardens to picnic under the cherry blossom trees, having fun in the knowledge that the blossom's display lasts only a short while. There's a certain poignancy, don't you think, in this short-lived celebration? There are so many spring festivals around the world, from all different belief systems. For example, there's *Imbolc*, a Celtic pagan fire festival held at the beginning of February and associated with fertility; and *Easter*, a Christian festival traditionally celebrating the resurrection of Christ, but now pregnant with the symbolism of new life in the form of images of spring flowers, chicks, eggs and so on.

What else signifies spring in our lives? The annual spring clean of our homes. I never quite understood the point of the tradition of the spring clean. As a teenager, I would complain to my mother saying, "Why do we have to take *everything* out of the cupboards, wipe all the shelves and then put *everything* back in again—and in its proper place?" It all seemed quite pointless, since no one would see inside the cupboards I would argue. I do have a better appreciation for it now and can understand it to be a deep clean of all areas of the home, the seen and the unseen! It's a freshening up at the start of a new year, a clearing away of old energy to make space for the new. It's the ever-present birth-preservation-death-rebirth cycle of all life on earth. This is the eternal rhythm of the seasons, of the moon, of our thoughts, of our breath. Everything about life on earth is constant change. We take a new breath, it is sustained, before being exhaled ready for the next breath (birth-preservation-death-rebirth). We have a thought, it stays in our mind for a few seconds, then dissipates before the next thought appears (birth-preservation-death-re-birth). All of our thoughts, words and acts undergo this same process. Think about that and you will see that it's true! That's why the imagery of the eternal cycle of the seasons forms an essential part of the structure of *Soul Murmurs*.

Even as a relatively recent yogi on the spiritual path, I can nevertheless understand the link between a physical spring clean and one on an emotional or spiritual level. If we want to be clean on the inside, we need to get rid of the dross: all those bad habits and negative thought patterns; all those attachments to things and people that we once believed would bring us happiness; all the hours spent in useless activity simply to fill times of boredom. I talk about this process of compassionate self-analysis in my book, *Acts of Kindness from Your Armchair*. This process of self-reform leads us along the pathway to peace and is both an inner and outer journey. The inner journey is one of renouncing bad habits and behaviors and replacing them with positive alternatives. Maintaining this practice is a major step in bringing about peace when all around is in turmoil. Once we've "cleaned up our act", we're ready for the outer journey. This is a shift in focus away from the ego towards acting for the sake of others. We are indeed doing a "spiritual" spring-clean, the ultimate goal of which is to think of and put others first above ourselves. And, by helping others I've found that we really do help ourselves!

Light is also an important symbol of spring. We talk of there being "light at the end of the tunnel", and I suppose the darkness of winter is merely an absence of light, or an absence of our ability to perceive the light, for it is never really extinguished; it simply changes its form. In spring, just as the natural world is awakening after those long days of winter darkness, so we also awaken to bring more light into our bodies, enveloping us like a soft cocoon. We venture outdoors more often; we tidy up the garden ready for spring flowers; we delight in the first buds which appear on plants and trees; we take in life-giving fresh oxygen from the air during walks in nature; we leave behind the heavy nourishing food of winter and start to eat lighter, fresher meals. In all these ways, we bring more light into our bodies. As we begin to enlighten ourselves in this way, we may also be imbued with a renewed determination in our spiritual practice and growth: physically, mentally, emotionally and spiritually. There is so much to be thankful for in this season of rebirth! At this time of plenty, we can plant the seeds of our aspirations and watch them grow, make cleaner, greener choices and choose to cherish all life.

The poems and prose of spring are full of light and optimism for the days ahead; verse and affirmations of friendship, gratitude, devotion and reflection; and a wonderful article with practical suggestions on how to imbue your life with more kindness and compassion at Easter-time. These first poems reflect my awakening wonder and awe at the Divine at work in the natural world. They mirror my gradual progress on the spiritual path from someone previously disgruntled with God and content to live a materialistic life, to a little child finding herself irresistibly drawn to return to Him. They speak of my inner peace, innocent joy and growing love for the Creator, which initially took me by surprise. I wasn't expecting my life to turn out this way—but I'm so very glad that it has! Let these words inspire and uplift you this spring. I hope that you too will be filled with renewed wonder for the natural world and God. I leave you with an affirmation for spring:

I will plant the seeds of my aspirations
And watch them grow with each passing day.

I See You Now

(where it all began, first published in *Kindred Spirit* magazine, August 2016)

This was the first poem penned from my hand. One evening in February 2016, poems began to come into my mind, usually as I meditated, and often as I dropped off to sleep. I remember complaining to my meditation teacher that I was having difficulty quietening my mind to meditate because poetry kept coming through. She advised me to go with it and let the words out. Now I am free to feel the joy in every word which seeps out from this connection to a higher state of being. I know that the more I flex this poetic muscle, the deeper, fuller and rounder the words will become, as I write about things which matter to me. I hope my words will also touch others. "I See You Now" was inspired by the walk that I used to take every day in the woods near my home. I didn't appreciate its full beauty then, but now that I am no longer able to walk far, I replay the trail in my mind's eye and can experience the beauty bursting out of every pore of this natural masterpiece: the sun filtering through the trees in the woods, the waters of the stream sparkling like diamonds, the forest floor carpeted with luxurious spring flowers. Such beauty all around. I see the Divine in all aspects of the natural world now; I feel peace and contentment in the simple things in life, the things that really and truly matter. It wasn't always so.

I spent so many years immersing myself in the sensory pleasures of the world, in the acquisition of beautiful things and in filling every moment with "must-have" experiences. I believed this was the way to happiness. And these things can bring us happiness—for a short while. Then dissatisfaction returns, so we need to aim higher, acquire/experience more, bigger, better and more often, in order to achieve the same "high". I know now that this emotional roller-coaster has misery as its ultimate destination. I created these sensory pleasures to try to fill a void that I instinctively felt inside.

I lived this lifestyle for a good many years and I believe it was rooted in a core belief of not being good enough. Many of us share this core belief. I tried to be like other people who were more popular, richer or funnier, believing that I too would be magically endowed with these properties. The chase of new possessions soon became more exciting than owning the objects themselves and then not even the chase could fill the void within. I realize with hindsight that there was a spiritual malaise growing inside me like a cancer, eating away at my happiness and health. I had removed myself from God many years before, believing He was irrelevant in my life. It struck me that this could be the underlying cause of all my symptoms. And so, once I had planted my feet firmly down on the road of spiritual practice and meditation, I started to recognize the Divine in others—in everyone and everything. And my increasing joy gradually began to melt away the spiritual sickness within!

Retraining the senses to experience the delights of the natural world has been a vital step for me in filling this inner void with light. I have discovered that it is these natural Divine creations which bring lasting joy. It's great to take time out from your day, pause for a while and notice the Divine at work in the natural world around you. It's like wakening up from a dream or wiping away the condensation from the car windscreen: you suddenly see things more clearly and wonder why you couldn't do so before! It's magical.

I see You now
In the flowing waters of the stream
Brighter and clearer than any diamond.

I hear You now
In the silence of my heart
Louder and richer than any song.

I feel You now
In the wind caressing my face
Sweeter and more tender
Than a lover's touch.

I taste You now
In the raindrops of an April shower
More refreshing than
A morning cup of tea.

I smell You now
In the bluebells and snowdrops
Of the forest.
More exquisite and uplifting
Than any perfume.

I see You now.
I see You now.

TODAY: Take time out from your busy day to really notice the natural world around you. Use your senses of sight, hearing, smell and touch. The world is truly magical if you pause to experience it!

The Blackbird

There he stands
At the curtain-call of day
When dusk's sweet light
Comes into play.
The telegraph post
His roost of choice.

Territory surveyed
With sharp, beady eyes
Sweeping like searchlights
Across the terrain.
Authority conveyed
With head held high
And dark ruffled coat
Buttoned up to the throat.

He steadies his voice
And croons a refrain
To the coming moonlight.
Singing his lullaby
With soft delight
Soothing the locale for the night.

The Blackbird: a simple reminder
Not to judge with our eyes,
For his plain exterior belies
The beauty of his song:
The melodic strains
Of an Angel's refrain.

What a beautiful gift for us all!
Until tomorrow, my friend.

TODAY: When you notice yourself judging someone solely by their outer appearance, stop. We've all been there, so you don't need to remonstrate with yourself over this ingrained habit of judgement. Instead, make a promise today that you will change to a new, positive habit of understanding. Try to see behind the exterior "mask" that we humans like to wear and see the soul that lies within. Each of us has our struggles and challenges in life, which we try to hide behind our masks. Treat others as you would like to be treated and be kind!

A Sunny Day in the North

What a beautiful, sunny day!
A cosmic blessing
On the rainy north.
The air seems to sigh
And the spaces
Between branches shimmer.
As the contraction
In my body eases and melts
With the warming caress
Of the sun's gentle rays.

Daffodils nod and bounce
An outward show
Of their inner dance of joy.
They peer round to observe
This object of beauty in the sky
Which beams its benevolent
Smile on us all.

The growing joy within me
Awakens the inner child
Who wants to run and skip,
Make daisy chains
Lying in a field of tall grass,
Watching shapes in the clouds
As they meander,
Unhurried, like my past.

"Have patience," I tell myself,
"For the sun's time is limited
And the chill yet prevails."
But summer is knocking

On the creaking wood
Around the door,
Whispering promises
Of lazy days
And warm bones ahead.

There's no such thing as bad weather,
only inappropriate clothing.
– Norwegian saying

We're accustomed to rain in Scotland. However, it's taken me so many years to come to an appreciation of the velvet-soft droplets falling from the sky. Plants and trees, and indeed all life relies on water to thrive. The wind which often accompanies the rain blows away the stale air making way for new life and energy to rush in. And if you have never stepped outside after a rain shower to smell the air, you ought to! So fresh and clean, it seems as if the plants are sighing with relief and pleasure! No artificial fragrance could truly capture its essence. There is a cleansing of spirit which takes place when we walk in softly falling rain: cool droplets landing on skin thirsty for moisture; refreshing peace in acceptance of this gift of life.

TODAY: Here are 3 things you can do to embrace nature:

- Love and respect your own part of the world;
- Thank Mother Nature for all the gifts She bestows upon us;
- Give something back (be kind to animals, use chemical-free products, sow wild seeds etc.).

The Bothy: a short story

PART ONE: The Forest

Thick snow crunched underfoot as Jim quickened his pace through the forest towards the clearing ahead. His eyes winced against the glaring sun piercing a sky of cobalt blue. Cheeks flared red with the intense cold which clung like a second skin. This was the coldest winter for a long time, he thought, as he gave an involuntary shiver, wrapping both arms around his chilled body. He knew he was close though.

He remembered she'd told him, "A couple of hundred yards or so after the clearing. For heaven's sake, go there, and find yourself." "It'll clear your head," she'd reminded him, "help you make sense of things again."

If only it were that simple, he muttered under his breath through cold-numbed lips, shoving both hands deep into the pockets of his all-weather jacket. She'd bought him it for his 50th birthday last year to encourage him to do more walking! Well, he'd been walking for just over an hour.

He had to admit she had a point. He had been feeling pretty lost these past few months. Blowing out his frustration with puffs of icy breath, he heard the buzzard's eerie call as it soared overhead as if pointing him in the right direction. Carving his way through the trees, he knocked off excess snow from his boots each time he stepped over a fallen log or leapt across a small stream which seemed to emerge from nowhere. He couldn't put a finger on what was behind this lost feeling he'd been experiencing. His job was fine. His relationship with his wife was fine. The kids were doing fine at university. Everything was fine.

"Was that it?" he thought. "Was I expecting more than fine? And what was so wrong with that anyway?"

Finally, it came into view. The "bothy"—a cabin made of stone and wood—nestled in the valley between two sides of an ancient ice-hewn fracture in the landscape. A few tentative smoke whirls rose from its little chimney sitting atop a roof of grey slate tiles. The walls were thick stone with one small window to the front to keep in as much heat as possible. In summer, it would have looked impossibly pretty, he thought, as he ventured nearer.

The smoke signaled that it was occupied. Jim swore inwardly to himself. He'd wanted to be alone there.

"Wasn't that the point?" he fumed. "Didn't you have to be alone to find yourself?"

His legs made to turn back, but his mind said, "Just go in and say hello and then you can leave." It wouldn't do to be rude… (To be continued.)

Winding Roads

Winding roads and lumpy hills
Lined by crowds of daffodils
Cheering on the weary traveler
"Not long now!" they cry.

Snow-crested mountains
Stand strong and serene
A majestic backdrop
To this beguiling scene:

Ochre heather and grey-colored scree
Trees clinging on at odd degrees
Ancient rocks clad in moss against the cold
Respite for travelers in days of old.

We are intruders in this landscape
Yet it seems a part of me—
Our shared heritage and history.
But this land belongs to all, not some.
Softly winding roads leading us home.

Seedlings of the Mind

During our meditation group this week, as it was a new moon, we set our intentions for the coming month and offered them up to the Universe. What does this mean and why do we do this at a new moon? The moon holds an incredible attraction for me in all its phases, and this attraction becomes "magnetic" halfway through its cycle. The lunar cycle is what we call the moon's orbit around the Earth, and what we see of the moon is the part that is illumined by the sun. The moon also serves as a spiritual symbol of the continuous cycle of life on Earth, forever in a state of change, but continuous and eternal.

Many of us feel such a strong lunar pull when it is at its fullest in the night sky. The traditional (non-scientific) explanation for this has been that because we humans are composed of water to a large extent (at least 50%), and, because the moon has such a strong effect on the tides on Earth, so also does its influence extend to our bodies. Whether you ascribe to this theory or not, for me personally I can affirm that I become very unsettled, agitated, "wired but tired" as I put it around this time. I sleep much less, rising in the middle of the night to write. For me it's a time of increased creativity. I might also add that I (along with many other teachers) have witnessed an increase in hyperactivity among students in the classroom around the time of the full moon!

But let's return to the new moon (often called the dark moon), which lies at the opposite end of the spectrum if you like to the full moon (the moon's phase is generally speaking: new, waxing, full, waning, new). When we think about it, the new moon is the time when our moon is not visible in the sky. It marks the beginning of its rebirth. It is also a return to emotional calmness for those of us who have experienced increased agitation during the fullest phase of the moon. And, just as we set annual intentions at the start of a new year, many astrologers, pagans and shamans among others believe that the time of the new moon is an optimum moment to "go within" and set intentions for the coming month. To start afresh with a new beginning. What do we want to achieve this month? How are we going to bring this about?

The new moon is therefore a time of hope and of looking forwards. At our meditation group, as we were setting our intentions for the coming month, I was reminded of the vegetable seedlings I had planted the week before, and which I was tenderly nurturing. I thought we really should do likewise with the seeds of our aspirations: not try to force them but nurture them gently and have faith that they will be realized. This last point is what is meant by "offering them up to the Universe". Here's the poem I wrote after meditation.

New Moon.
Time of hope and renewal
For planting the seeds
Of our aspirations
And watching them grow
With each passing day.

Tenderly nurture these seedlings
Of your mind
Do not force them
Lest they stretch and fail
But sprinkle them daily
With the fairy dust
Of your will.

Imagine your intentions
Embodied in reality
Walking among us
With the awe of new life.

TODAY: Set an intention for today or this week. What would you like to achieve? What steps can you take to achieve it? Write them down and keep them with you as a reminder.

Wants and Needs

One spring day I sat outside in the garden nourishing my body with a healing infusion of the sun's warming rays. Cup of tea in hand, I was immersed in the scene playing out around me; completely entranced and "in the moment". Who would have thought that sitting on a plain wooden bench in the garden on a spring morning would equate to absolute bliss and contentment? If you'd asked me years ago, I would have said, "Not me! How boring would that be!" I feel blessed that my outlook on life has changed so radically in the intervening years. Illness has given me the space and time to really rediscover who I am behind all the masks of personality and character traits that I have worn in the past, and I am so grateful for the lessons I have learned through these health challenges. Some of these are compassion for others, discovering where true, lasting contentment lies, reconnecting with God and so on.

There are times, however, when I take my blessings for granted. We all do this. We focus on what we can't do, not on what we can; we engulf ourselves in what we don't have and not in what we have; we ask: "Why me?" instead of: "Why not me?" Lack of gratitude is simply a poor, learned habit which we can unlearn. We can replace these learned habits with a new, positive awareness of what we have in abundance in our lives (people, attributes, skills, possessions, services, and so on).

So, there I was sitting on the bench, feeling the sun gradually warm my body and the thought popped into my head that I was just like a cold-blooded lizard stretching out on a rock to warm up in the morning sun. The only thing on the lizard's mind is heating up his body to allow him to function. He is solely focused on the present moment. Can we say the same?

TODAY: Set an alarm on your phone or tablet to go off at regular intervals throughout the day. Each time it does so, pause what you are doing and say out loud something you are grateful for in your life. Express gratitude for a different thing each time! If you want, you can also write them down. These lists are wonderful to look back on from time to time (especially those times when you are feeling down) as a reminder of all the blessings in your life.

Sitting in the garden on my favorite seat
Warming my body in the sun's gentle rays
Like a lizard stretched out on a stone am I
Ingesting the heat in gluttonous sighs.

My blessings well up in me—
An emotional geyser about to pop
I've had a wonderful life this time around:
A plethora of loved ones
Food in abundance
Water in effulgence
Warm clothes, safe home. Love.
What did I do to deserve all this?

Notwithstanding all our wants,
What more could a person need?:
Respect for and from others
Purpose and reason to serve
Faith in the seen and unseen.

I have all these and more!:
Hope for the future and
Forgiveness of the past
Really living in the present
Relishing each moment.

My soul uplifted, the body recharged
I stretch like the lizard and
Scamper off to enjoy the day.

My M.E. Story: by Anita Neilson

(first published in *ME Essential* magazine, Issue 143, Winter 2017)

I don't like to be identified by my health conditions, but I want to include this article about M.E. and Fibromyalgia and how I cope with them in my life. They fall into the category of "invisible" conditions and as such many people can find them difficult to understand and empathize with. If someone has a blatant physical condition such as a broken leg, it's easy to give them sympathy and support, isn't it? Yet if they have overwhelming fatigue and chronic pain in muscles, tissues, bones and joints, exacerbated by the least activity, these are not visible symptoms and sufferers can easily look "perfectly healthy" to others, on a good day. Just as mental health is becoming a topic more widely discussed in public, so do I hope that other invisible conditions will follow suit in this positive vein; for don't we all have some pain which is invisible to others? It may be physical, mental, emotional or spiritual, but we all need to undergo suffering throughout our lives as part of the process of growth. Suffering has brought me the blessing of increased understanding of and compassion for others who are in pain. It has allowed me the space and time to rediscover who I really am behind all the masks. Saint Teresa of Avila said that God calls souls back to Him in many ways, and that "sometimes He calls souls by means of sickness or troubles." I believe that there's a purpose behind all our experiences on Earth and having spent many fruitless years trying to control this purpose I came to the realization that we are *not* in control of it. He is. Here is the article. I hope you find it helpful.

I would describe myself as a "fairly stressed secondary school teacher" when M.E. (Chronic Fatigue Syndrome) came to visit with me in 2008 and it remains a tolerated guest today. Absolutely exhausted by morning coffee break, I had to push myself on to finish another day, all the while bumping into desks and doorframes, head spinning whenever I stood up, mind going completely blank when trying to teach—not ideal with a classroom full of unsettled teenagers. I deteriorated quite quickly after that, eventually becoming unable to work or do any of the hobbies I had once enjoyed. And so, I found myself at home, bewildered and depressed. Of course, it took years to have this strange illness diagnosed. Then, after a major operation in 2010, Fibromyalgia (F.M.) came along bearing the "gifts" of chronic pain and yet more fatigue. But like visitors who have stayed past their welcome, I have now accepted their presence in my life, adopted new ways of living with them and even acknowledged the gifts which came along with them. That's not to say this hasn't been a long journey and that it's not still ongoing—it has been a long journey and it is still ongoing. I've just decided to come at it from a different angle.

I've slowly learned to view chronic illness as a grieving process. You grieve for the person you once were and go through the stages of grief: 1. Denial and isolation; 2. Anger; 3. Bargaining; 4. Depression; and 5. Acceptance. For many years, I searched for alternative diagnoses, any explanation for my symptoms that was more acceptable to me. Then I became angry—the Why Me? Stage—before realizing that none of us is the person we once were 5, 10, even 20 years ago. Each of us has our challenges to face in life and if we didn't have any challenges, how would we grow? Then came bargaining with God: "If I change my ways, will you take this illness from me?" and so on! Depression has been a well in my psyche for a good many years, and one down which I have regularly fallen.

Now, nine years later, I have at last accepted M.E. and F.M. as being part of the new me, and I'm content with that. This doesn't mean I have resigned myself to a life of negativity and pain. Far from it! But the years of struggling were like carrying two heavy suitcases with me wherever I went. Renouncing this struggle, the suitcases have been dropped and left where they fell, leaving a lighter, brighter, happier me. The space within, long darkened by frustration, anger, spite, self-pity and selfishness has gradually been re-illumined with patience, love, understanding, selflessness and compassion for others. This change in focus from inward-looking to outward acting has been the biggest catalyst for change in my physical, emotional, mental and spiritual health.

The second change has been rediscovering my love for writing, which I'd long since forgotten about in the intervening years of career, life's challenges and ill-health. Since the onset of M.E. I've been mostly housebound and this led me to feel unable to contribute to the world. I didn't want to be an eco-warrior or do big, visible acts of kindness on a national or global scale, but I wanted to feel that my life had purpose. No longer able to hold down a job, which on reflection had become my whole identity, I felt lost and didn't know who I was any longer. This got me thinking that there must be others in similar circumstances who also felt bereft of purpose and seemingly unable to make a meaningful contribution to the world because of illness or physical or social isolation. And so, I started to blog and write poetry, not knowing if anyone out there was reading it, but just doing it because it gave my life purpose. So really, at the start, writing was a selfish activity for me; it was about helping me, distracting myself from pain, fatigue and frustration. Yet, something so wonderful started to happen as the first year went by and I realized that I wanted to write to help other people feel good about themselves and distract *them* from their pain. It made me feel good to do this. It might seem an odd thing to say, but the truth was that I finally understood that I could help myself by helping others.

It's important for us all to know that we can improve our mental and emotional well-being by finding a new purpose in life. This can help to reduce levels of stress and anxiety which in turn may also have a positive effect on our physical well-being. In my case I know that stress increases the physical symptoms of M.E. and F.M., so anything I can do to minimize this, I will grasp with both hands! We are capable of so much more than we at first believe. We are stronger and kinder than we think. We can all, regardless of our limitations, make a positive contribution to the world around us. I truly believe this and I wish you well.

TODAY: Think of some way that you can help others. It could be in your thoughts, words or actions. Remember, if you are housebound and/or socially isolated, there are still many ways you can be of service to the world, and trust me when I say that helping others really does distract us from our own challenges in life!

A New Stitch of Friendship

I am knitting a square of the
Blanket of the world
The wool in my fingers
Soft yet strong
A perfect network
Of thought and form.

There are mossy greens
And chocolatey browns
Tough and hardwearing
Like the good Scottish soil.
There are dazzling purples
And sun-kissed yellows
Sparkling gems
Of gorse and heather.

Each click of needles and
Winding wool round
Creates a new stitch of friendship
A binding connection:
Beauty through kindness and
Strength through compassion.

The grey and white clouds
Mask the blues of the sky
Soothing my soul
Like a sateen lullaby.

The blacks of the birds' wings are
Dotted now and again
But there is no wool to convey
Their sweet refrain.

Each day I knit,
Binding the square
With my love
Forming connections
Below and above.
Each day I knit,
Though my fingers
May ache
Each day will I knit,
For the need is still great.

TODAY: Try to remember that all life on earth is interconnected, and that what you think, say and do *will* affect others. What can you do today to encourage connection with someone else whom you see as different?

I am Complete

If I tortured myself with regrets—which I don't—I think one of them would be not making more effort to nurture friendships early on in my adult life. Being an A-type personality (someone who is very driven and determined to succeed) led to me being ferociously competitive in all areas of life: work, boyfriends, material acquisitions, physical fitness, and outward appearances. The problem with being very driven is that it can eventually lead to loneliness which creeps up on you unawares. Many A-type personalities are simply too busy trying to be the best at everything that they don't see the value in allotting time to friendships. This was further complicated by the fact that in my mind, I was competing with other women for available men; I wanted to have lovely possessions (clothes, car etc.), and a beautifully decorated home; I had to be the best in the yoga class, the fittest in the aerobics class. I socialized with my sisters and with colleagues and considered this to be a good way to live, until the realization hit in my early 40s that I had no real friends who weren't related to me, married to me or who didn't work with me. Oh dear. This came as a bit of a bombshell.

At the same time, I began reading self-help books and started meditation classes. As I gradually learned the many techniques and knowledge for leading a more spiritual and kinder life, I intuitively recognized that up to this point I had not been a very kind person. How did this unkindness manifest itself? Well, let's see. I talked about people behind their back, I suppose in a vain effort to make myself feel superior by making them appear inferior. I was too quick to judge others simply by outward appearances. How arrogant I was, thinking myself better than others. I was irritated by those with disabilities or mobility problems if they got in my way and slowed me down. Shocking isn't it! It is cathartic to admit to these negative habits of thinking and behaving, because I know with certainty now that there is a better way of being and doing.

I can't express how much my life has changed since I started learning to put kindness to the forefront of my life. It has brought friends to me; it has brought opportunities; it has brought the blessing of ill-health, which has allowed me to develop compassion for those who live with disabilities or chronic illnesses in life. My good(God)-ness. Life is good now! Here is my poem about friendship. It's full of the child-like glee of joy at the simple things in life, which are the most important after all.

TODAY: If you're a competitive person like me, remember that everything we have (looks, personality, possessions, skills and so on) is on loan to us for this lifetime. We can't take any of it with us when our time comes to leave the earth. Are these things really so much more important than allowing love into your heart? Here's the poem:

I am complete
I am replete
I open the door on this life
And gifts in abundance
Come tumbling out:
Love for living
Joy in giving
Health and well-being
Bounty beyond all my needs.

But friendship holds me high
With encouragement to fly
"Look at me!" I squeal
As I soar in the sky
Like a kite on a blustery day
Vulnerable yet full of joy
Free to be me
Supported by the filaments
Of companionable love.

Come let me heal you

Come let me heal you
She whispers in the breeze
Let the salt air renew you
And the soft sand imbue
Your flagging spirit with life.

Come walk beside me
She beckons in my ear
Let the freshness of my realm
Invigorate your cells
And the rhythm of my heartbeat
Soothe all your ills.

Come let me heal you
Breathe in and out
Come let me heal you
Look within and without
Come let me heal you
Renew you, uplift you
Come let me heal you
My Beloved Child of Light.

♫ *Listen to the audio version of the poem.*

Thou Art Mine!

I was watching a television drama about the Bronte sisters and afterwards the thought came to me of how someone like Charlotte Bronte would have written a poem "in old-fashioned language", as I put it, about the mountains. These are the words which came through, so seamlessly and quickly that I had to race to write them down lest they disappear without a trace! I love it and I hope you do too.

O mountainous glory thou art mine!
Whose velvet carpeting affords
Soft repose to weary limbs.

Whose lithesome wind
Caresses each pore,
Gladly surrendering.

Where an outstretched hand
May touch Infinity
And embrace it within.

O mountainous wonder thou art mine!
Whose poets and artists
Have long pondered life
And sought to imbue it with light.

Whose skylines are traced
With creative imaginings
Preserving God's masterpiece in time.

Misty Mornings

I was trying to sleep one afternoon, but the beginning of this piece kept repeating itself in my mind, a sure sign that I should get up and write the words down lest I lose them as quickly as they had arrived. I am entranced by early morning, the quiet time just before all the chaotic "human" action begins. Here are today's musings:

The mist hangs low across the field this early morn: an ethereal backdrop to the grand play of life; a silken web of silence spun by Nature's thread. All the supporting characters are already in place. The trees stand stock still, a verdant frame if you will to the enfolding picture, with their delicate branches trailing to touch those of their neighbors, as if wishing to hold hands. A couple of roe deer graze in their usual spot in the far corner of the field, ears, head and tail popping up at the slightest sound. And the birds—both garden and woodland—are rousing, taking their roll call, yet still too drowsy to venture out for food.

There linger a few man-made traces in the pink-smeared sky—evidence of recent holidays abroad and business trips. Life in the fast lane. If only it were as easy for us to fly as it is for our avian friends! The swallows who dart and swoon so gracefully and in perfect unison, or the woodpecker with his comical bounce, seeming as if he will tumble out of the sky at any moment, or finally the great majestic buzzard who languidly circles in the blue. His eerie call echoes through the treetops, attracting families of crows to rise in ambush of this dangerous intruder.

My neighbor (some 20 years my senior and hardier than a lifelong North Sea fisherman) is walking his dogs. Rico, the soppy Rottweiler, who sits on your feet and leans into your legs for a cuddle, and little tiny Rosie, a fawn-colored terrier, barrel-round and waddling, with the cutest face to bring a smile to the gloomiest of hearts. I wave to them through the glass. "Well now," I turn and say to my own two dogs, "let's take our places, girls. Today's play has begun!"

TODAY: Try not to let the drama of life's ups and downs get to you. Just treat them like scenes in a play or movie. Keep yourself a little more detached from the action. This helps to balance your mood and steady your emotions, leading to a calmer, happier you!

Peeling the Onion

Peeling an onion
Brings tears to the eyes
As the bulb fragments
And each layer subsides
So pain is released
With each slice of the knife.

Yet life is an ever-changing menu
Of movement and moment;
Each course is a quest
On the spiritual path
The next sweeping the last
With a grateful refrain
Carrying us forward like Gawain
On his steed. Fear not the pain
In life's great repast!

Release tears of joy
When peeling the onion
For as each layer is shed
So the whole is strengthened
Taking us closer
To the core of our being.

Advance bravely on your steed,
Dear Knight
Give thanks for the past;
Have faith in the future
And embrace this inner quest
To the God-spark at the center.

TODAY: For us to progress spiritually, we need to get rid of our bad habits of thinking and doing. Each time we carry out this inner work, we are peeling away another layer of "dross" in order to reach the perfect soul at the center. Think of a bad habit you would like to get rid of and start work on this today. Every time it manifests itself, recognize it and take action to substitute it with the opposite, positive habit or quality. There may be tears along the way, but it will be worth it.

Perfect Reflections

I see Your light shine, Lord,
In the eyes of a child
Innocent reflection of You.
I see Your light shine
In all new-born life
Purest perfections of truth.

Your light shines clearly
In charitable deeds
Through kindness
And compassion to all.
Your light shines clearly
Through branches of trees
And the scent of the rain
As it falls.

Help me see Your light
In the killer and the swindler
For my judgement of them
Rends my own light dimmer.
Help me see Your light
In the cheat and the sinner
For I condemn myself
When I condemn another.

Show me Your light
In the evil deeds of men
For dost not evil
Merely cover the good in them?
Show me Your light
In hurtful, vengeful words
For dost not pain

Merely cover forgotten love?
Give me the strength, Lord,
To proclaim what is true:
That we are *all*
Perfect Reflections of You.

Six Steps to Easter Kindness

*Let's take a break from poetry. Here's an article about
how to show kindness at Easter time.*

Kindness is our natural state of being and it is essential to nour-
ish this innate capacity throughout the year. However, when we
gather together at times of celebration such as Easter, it's espe-
cially important to show love and kindness to ourselves and oth-
ers and give thanks for all our blessings. Outlined below are the
6 steps to Easter kindness (E.A.S.T.E.R.) that all of us can take to
lighten and brighten our lives and the world around us.

E for Elimination
Lent (the six weeks leading up to Easter Sunday) is a time of
renunciation, when many of us choose to forgo a bad habit (per-
haps an overindulgence in food or alcohol, excessive swearing
etc.). The best way I have found to temper fear and temptation
is through love and kindness. Here are some ways to show kind-
ness to yourself and others under the first heading of Elimination:

- Take some quiet time for yourself this Easter. In meditation
  or periods of rest, use the symbolism of the fire and ashes to
  hand over any bad habits of thought or behavior. Let them
  be consumed by a spiritual fire to be recreated as purity and
  positivity. Continue in this new positive vein and eliminate
  them permanently!
- Have a physical clear out of your home and/or office. Get
  rid of unnecessary clutter to give yourself more space and
  clarity of thought. Donate items to charities, give other items
  away, sell some you no longer want and if you can afford to
  do so, give the money to charity.
- Encourage your children to donate an item for other chil-
  dren to enjoy.

A for Acceptance

Accept others for who they are and not who you want them to be. We hold mental images of perfection in our minds about our loved ones and are disappointed when they do not attain these high standards. Next time you are about to have an argument with your partner about the mess or not taking the trash out, for example, stop and say to yourself: "I'd rather have the mess/the trash than not have him/her." Keep saying this each time. We all have our ingrained habits and opinions which are very difficult to change, and it is pointless trying to control people. Let them be who they are and take delight in your differences!

S for Sharing

The giving of eggs has been used by Christians around the world at Easter time to symbolize new life and also the empty tomb of Jesus after he rose from the dead. Here are some additional ways to share your good fortune with others this Easter:

- buy an extra Easter egg to give to either a food bank or a neighbor;
- give your time to someone this Easter;
- give other symbols of new life, such as plant seedlings, to a local nursery or primary school.
- Easter is a fun festival for children. Consider making a donation to a charity such as UNICEF which protects all children around the world.

T for Transforming

Spare a thought this Easter time for people who are struggling—mentally, physically, emotionally. A few words of encouragement can transform someone's day (or life!). Here are two schemes which you might like to take part in: sendkidstheworld. com and moreloveletters.com. The first is a simple idea of sending postcards to sick children from around the world to light up their day during some pretty dark times. This is easily done from home and you can involve your children, encouraging them to think of others as they design or purchase their own postcards to send. Moreloveletters.com is similar, but in this case, the website hosts "love" letter requests, perhaps from a neighbor of an elderly person who would benefit from a letter or two, or from a college student living away from home for the first time and struggling to engage with campus life who would similarly benefit from some words of encouragement. Two very worthwhile causes, enabling you to spread compassion and kindness easily through the written word. And if you struggle to write, remember there are many voice-activated apps which will convert the spoken word to text!

E for Energizing

Analyze what needs reenergizing in your life. Is it your work/life balance; health and fitness; spiritual health; relationships with family, friends or work colleagues. Choose one aspect every week and concentrate on ways in which this can be reenergized. Here are some suggestions to get you started:

- go for refreshing, revitalizing walks after work to clear your mind;
- physically speak to colleagues sometimes rather than always sending e-mails;
- go to the yoga or meditation classes which had caught your eye;
- help out at your church food bank or other charitable group;
- give people your full attention when they are talking to you, looking them in the eye.

R for Remembering

After an Easter celebration, remember others who are not as fortunate as you. Below are some easy ways to do this:

- Donate some chocolate or flowers to a local nursing home where many residents rarely or never receive visitors or presents. How kind to remember them in your thoughts and acts!
- Encourage the children to accompany you so that they may learn to be respectful of and thoughtful to the older generation.
- Remember the ancestors who have gone before. Think of the gifts they bestowed on you (physical attributes, financial legacy, good upbringing and so on) and share this gratitude with the next generation.

All of us can be happier and more fulfilled by allowing kindness to come to the forefront of our daily lives. When we remember to think of others, it fills us with gratitude for all our blessings. Whatever you are doing this Easter, I wish you a joyful time of celebration, love and kindness.

Angel by my Side

When I stop doing and sit quietly
Just being, I feel you by my side
Trusted friend and guide.

Towering over me
Your wings enfolding me
In a loving embrace
As a parent to a child.

My scalp tickles at your touch
Causing smiles of surrender
All over this body.
Such benevolence! Such grace!

Your breath pours over me
Soothing my muscles
Loosening these joints
Quietening my mind
Unlocking the Soul.

Let your light course through me
Sending healing to all.
Give me strength to work with you
In service to all.
Be by my side always
To catch me when I fall.

The Holy Grail

The backdrop to this poem is The Grail Legend which has been the subject of many tales over the centuries. I was fascinated by the mystery of the Grail and studied its mediaeval French literature at university. It was said to be the chalice from the Last Supper, used to collect the blood of Christ as he hung on the cross at his Crucifixion, then brought to Britain by Joseph of Arimathea and hidden. Chretien de Troyes was the first to write about the Holy Grail in his *Conte del Graal* in the 12th century, the protagonist of which was Percival. The Knights of the Round Table were later reputed to have gone in search of it.

I believe the Grail is actually Christ's legacy on Earth: his teachings. I have spent many years looking around me, seeking happiness in many different ways. I have created man-made moments of joy to fill a lack within. That's where I feel many of us become trapped on the treadwheel of "must have more, must have better". If acquiring more things and experiences becomes the be-all and end-all of our lives, we will never find true, lasting happiness! Jesus said to his followers when they worried about material things: "But seek ye first the kingdom of God and His righteousness; and all these things shall be added unto you" (Matthew 6:33).

In other words, look inwards to find lasting happiness. Once I did this, I found that I no longer craved the sensory pleasures as much as I once did. A life based on must-have experiences, endless holidays to escape reality, spending money needlessly, anaesthetizing myself with alcohol or drugs and so on, was seen for what it was: hollow, soul-less. We can all make a positive change. If you connect with God through daily meditation; if you help others because it seems like the right thing to do; if you try every day to be a kinder, more understanding, less judgmental person, all your needs will be provided for. This has been my personal experience.

TODAY: Think about all aspects of your life (employment, home life, leisure and so on) and prepare a mental list of the ways in which you can use your God-given skills and attributes in service to others. Here is the poem:

What secret treasure is this
Which Percival sought on his quest:
A chalice, a relic, the blood of Christ?

The Grail is no object to be found
But a sacred knowledge to be unwound.

Seek within for the Divine spark of love
And there shall you find it.
A heart overflowing with the spirit of Christ
The lifeblood of service to all.

Aurora

The air is so still
Life seems held in stasis
In hushed anticipation
Of the day to come.

A soft pink streak
Hugs the horizon
One final embrace
Of the dawn
Before the moon
Hands the reins to the sun.

A few tentative birdcalls
Span the divide
Melting away
In the day's mellow hues.

I take in a lungful
Of this life-giving breath
Charging my cells
For another day on Earth.

Thank you, Divine Mother
For the gifts you bestow
Not least among them,
The glorious dawn.

♫ *Listen to the audio version of the poem.*

Loving Thy Neighbor

This is a lovely, simple prayer which you could print off and keep in your wallet or purse or pin it to your wall. Spend a few minutes in reflection during the day thinking about others and about how you can help them. There are many ways to help. Here are some examples:

- by your thoughts (sending love to those in need);
- your words (being understanding, non-judgmental);
- your acts (living by example; philanthropy);
- by giving your time;
- sharing your expertise;
- donating money and so on.

Divine Father,
Teach me the value of
Kindness to others.
Show me the merit of
Loving my neighbor.
Help me to serve with
No thought of reward.
These things I pray
From this day forward.

Your Grace

I have been meditating with the same group for almost 4 years now. We sometimes have a light lunch afterwards, and as we sat together today, I felt my heart expand, full of love and appreciation for these new friends and kindred spirits, and gratitude for the fellowship we share. Many people believe it's important to give thanks (Latin: *gratia*) to God before eating. In this way, we sanctify the act and affirm that everything we do, we owe solely to God. This prayer of thanks before eating is called *"a grace"*. This is the *grace* I wrote to express my love for all my friends, including my best friend, God.

TODAY: Why not pause before eating a meal and say a few words of gratitude (to God, the Universe, or whichever higher power you believe in) for the food you have before you; for all the people involved in bringing it to your table; and also spare a thought for those around the world who don't have such ready access to food.

> As we sit at table
> In blessed communion
> I gaze at the faces
> And my heart embraces
> The joyful refrain
> Of a nightingale's call.
>
> I give thanks for this
> Wonderful union
> Of dear friends,
> Spiritual sisters.
> Chatting and smiling,
> Lifting our spirits

Nourishing our souls
With the bread of life.

This table is our haven
Laden with food,
Lovingly prepared
And offered up in Your name.
Bless all who commune here
Lord, by Your Grace.

Shape me in Your image

Take me and shape me
In Your image, Lord.
Carry me and mold me
Never let go of me.
Help me to reason
With love and compassion:

If there are souls in pain
Help me comfort them.
If Your children are in need
Help me provide for them.
Of all wrong-doings
Help me forgive them.
For these things
You do for me
Day after day.

Shape me in Your image, Lord
And shower me
In the Heavenly Rays
Of Your Divine Perfection.

Under the Rainbow

Most of us go about our day connected to the physical, material world, experiencing life through our pseudo-self (the ego). The ego keeps us on the treadwheel of likes and dislikes, desires, and filling our life with experiences and possessions to try to feel happy. Yet, I know from experience that this happiness is short-lived. Being close to God is what brings me happiness now.

This poem is inspired by those moments when I feel close to Him when meditating. For me, connecting with my "real" Self (the soul) every day is massively beneficial to physical and emotional health. I am a learner on the path of Kriya yoga, learning breath and mantra practices from a meditation teacher and following the spiritual teachings and guidance of my guru, Paramahansa Yogananda. If this kind of practice seems overly burdensome to you, there are many mobile apps available that you can try to enable you to take even a few minutes' time-out from your busy day. Why not start today? This poem tries to describe the moments of bliss I sometimes experience, and the visual delights which can be perceived through the spiritual eye in the center of the brow during meditation and moments of stillness. I hope you enjoy it!

An enchantment
Through my scalp
Like a rainbow
Emerging from Source
Expanding and inspiring
Those held under its dome.

In this cocoon
I am and was
Lustrous threads

Of connectedness
To all that is.

In this world
I observe the other:
Beautiful, exciting,
Exhausting chaos.

In this moment,
There is no other:
An infusion of color
Dispersing in wonder
Showering my thoughts
In grace.

▶ *Watch the video poem.*

Wonderland

Beguiling reverie
Resplendent in color
Where dreams
Are the stuff
That life is made of.

Plugged-in reality
A virtual reflection
Of thought-in-action
Where magic
Knows no bounds.

This Universal Matrix
Providing the framework
For us to play and grow
Is a fairy-tale wonderland
Of light and shade
Highs and lows:

"Earth: The Greatest Show
In the Universe!"

Yet much as I relish
The delights of this world
I dream of the day
When my Prince will come
And awaken me
From this sleep-state
To live out Eternity
In that Other Realm,
Blissful and happy...
With Him at my side.

TODAY: Don't take life (and yourself) too seriously! We are all simply playing our role in this Divine drama of life on earth. Treat everyone you meet and everything that happens (good and bad) today as an opportunity to learn something and become a better person.

God Willing!

This poem was inspired by reading The Bhagavad Gita. I keep this sacred text (and wonderful teaching tool) by my bed and read a verse or two before sleep. One particular verse I read was about how we (over-) plan our lives and then expect everything to play out according to our plan. However, we forget that we are living to God's plan. So, the advice given is that by all means plan and go about your daily life, but don't be upset if the outcome differs from what you had envisaged. Perhaps you have something to learn from this different outcome? Furthermore, how can any of us really plan for the future since we don't know what it holds for us?

TODAY: Try to let go of the tight grip of control over all aspects of your life. It is very freeing to surrender and "go with the flow". Take just one aspect of your life which you like to control, perhaps punctuality, and ask yourself, "Why is it important that I arrive on time?" "Is it because I fear others' disapproval?" "If so, why is this?" Work on analyzing a different aspect of control each day and relinquish it to God and the Universe. It's amazing!

My "To Do" list
Overflows
With instructions
And commands,
Priorities, urgencies:
Satisfying all demands.

My mind
Paddles furiously
Spinning post-it notes
On plates

Everything is planned
To the minute
—Never late.

But the Universe
Throws us curve-balls
Which we can't
Anticipate.

So shall I plan
And order my day
Yet not despair at any delay,
Or change to the billing.

For all things shall happen
In good time—God Willing!

Let go of the Tug of War rope!

When I was younger, I would fall out with people almost daily. If I didn't get my own way, I would stomp away in a bad mood. I used to feel like the aggrieved person until I read somewhere many years later that this kind of behavior is in reality a type of soft bullying. If you think about it, bullying is forcing others to do your will, usually with an element of humiliation involved. This had been my learned behavior since childhood to get my own way, to feel elated, to feel in control, albeit temporarily. Why did I need to feel in control? Retrospect brings a little clarity perhaps. The second youngest of a large high-achieving family, my core belief was always "I'm not good enough". That's no excuse I realize, but it goes some way towards explaining why I reacted in this way. Yet, when we are on the receiving end of bad behavior, why is it so difficult for us to forgive the other party? Because our ego is wounded. It wants to be right and for others to be wrong.

What if we came at this from a different angle and adopted the assumption that there is no "right" or "wrong"; that both parties are simply on either end of the one line of truth. This makes sense to me, for one person's truth is another person's disbelief.

Just as in a game of Tug of War, we can only be victorious by bringing the other down. I no longer believe that this is how we should live our lives just so that we appear to be in the right.

There is another way. What would happen if we just let go of the rope? Agree to disagree and end the pointless tussling to and fro. Take delight in others' different opinions and ways of doing things. We don't need to fear that which is different, but rather embrace the amazing diversity of life on earth. And remember, we have lessons to learn from every single person we meet in life. What could you learn from the next person you come across!

Summer

Introduction to Summer:

What happy memories I have of long summer holidays when I was a child. We lived on the edge of a town, bordering open fields with countryside views as far as the eye could see. How I longed to be old enough and strong enough to walk the country lane leading up to the farm which framed the view at the top of the hill. I was desperate to see what lay on the other side! Memories of hazy days making daisy chains or running through the fields of barley almost as tall as I; of making up games to play with friends and staying out all day only returning home to eat. We delight in all of nature when we're children, don't we? It's sad that we leave behind this innocent joy when we get older and feel the huge societal pressure to become more sensible. I sometimes think that as we "grow up" in stature we "grow down" in our connection with the natural world. I can still clearly visualize these childhood memories—long walks along the beach, tiny frames buffeted by Atlantic winds; the pungent smell of silage being spread on fields, an aroma so strong it seemed to stick to our lungs; walking barefoot on grass and hot tarmac. When was the last time most of us walked barefoot on grass? It felt delicious. We'd be too worried about bacteria now!

Naturally, I have other less pleasant memories of childhood: falling off a tree-swing and injuring my spine; being harassed because of my religion; fighting with my siblings. Yet really, I have had a life crammed full of blessings and that's what I choose to focus on this summer and every other season of the year.

This season is the time of growth. Spring's heady enthusiasm and shoots of joy mellow now into a maturation of life, infused with the heady sights, smells and sounds of summer. Light grows daily in intensity and length. The haze of summer seems palpable at times, as if we could reach out and touch the aromatic "scentsations" which surround us. I am so blessed to live near to a meadow full of wild flowers and grasses, munched in turn by horses or deer. Even watching it from my window fills me with joy and lifts even the lowest mood. I may have passed the summer of my physical and mental life (I would describe myself as most definitely autumnal!) but spiritually I'm in summer. Deeper meditation, a willingness to help others and a determination to reform myself of bad habits and negative ways of thinking have all contributed to this more rounded awareness of the reality of life on Earth and our role within it. Summer sunlight at its strongest enables all life to flourish. Similarly, spiritual enlightenment enables our inner light to grow, and importantly, to then be shared with others, as if poured over them like a healing salve.

Let summer's words pour over and through you now, uplifting body, mind and spirit. From "The Beautiful Goodbye", a heartfelt remembrance of a dream visitation; celebratory poems of love, marriage, friendship; verse about summer storms, since I know that summer's heat and beauty is tempered with threatening storms. "The Storm's Coming" is one such poem. I wrote this sitting in the car parked outside a garage, waiting for my husband. The sky was growing darker and more ominous as the minutes ticked loudly past; a flagpole to my left insistently clinked against its supporting pole; the air, which moments earlier had seemed to envelop all life in a warm, hazy shimmer, now suffocated and throbbed. Tension was increasing, and I could almost feel the sparks of energy in the atmosphere. I knew the storm was coming and was in awe of the power of mother nature.

I love this duality about life on earth: light v. dark; storm v. calm; ignorance v. wisdom and so on. Each thought, emotion and habit has its opposite. For example, if we have never experienced what it is to be anxious, how would we really know what it was to be at peace? I've found this duality to be true in so many areas of my life. Like all of us, we need to go through challenges and trials in order to grow and be rewarded with a renewed appreciation of the good things in life, which we may previously have taken for granted.

In this section, you may also see a growing compassion for all life (poems such as "Liberty"), as well as an acknowledgement of the lessons we can learn from nature. "Flex" is one of my favorites about the beech tree in the meadow opposite which frames the view from my window. As I have health conditions— Fibromyalgia and M.E. (chronic fatigue syndrome)—which prohibit me from doing much activity within or out with the house, I do spend time each day gazing out at the ever-changing view, and the beautiful beech tree is the strong, steady stalwart, my constant companion. In windy days, I can hear her creaking as she flexes. I am inspired by her ability to be blown about by trials and yet return to her center afterwards with a strengthened core. That's how I want to live my life.

The Beautiful Goodbye

I woke up one morning not long after a dear friend had died. I had had a beautiful dream which I've since learned described as a "dream visitation". This is when a loved one who has passed comes to communicate with us while we are in the space between sleep and awake (in my case, just before waking). They choose this time because our rational mind and ego are not yet engaged but our spiritual, intuitive side is.

This dear friend, while in the physical body on earth, had the coldest hands due to heart problems; she hated having her photograph taken; and her home was full of rose potpourri. This beautiful dream gave me such a feeling of well-being, warmth, reassurance: LOVE. I will always remember every sensory detail of it, from the smell of rose, to the touch of her hand. She did not speak, but when she took my hand in hers, I exclaimed, "Oh, your hands are so warm!" She left me with the warmest embrace, and I immediately woke up my husband amidst tears of joy to tell him all about it. Whether she was visiting just to let us know that she was okay, or whether it was reassurance for the future (when my husband and then I both became seriously ill), I don't know, but it was simply, wonderfully magical! I hope you enjoy the poem.

TODAY: Enjoy every moment with loved ones and treat every experience as magical!

The touch of her hand
So cold in the living years
Now warmed my heart
Soft like a feather's whisper.

Her smile, so often
Hidden from gaze

Spoke now of joy.
No more trying to please,
Just being
In indescribable bliss.

We embraced,
Auras melding

Two souls knowing
They would meet again.

The scent of rose
Thick in the air
A souvenir of the
Beautiful goodbye.

I opened my eyes,
Wiped tears of joy
And smiled.

Surrender to the Flow

Bobbing about
On the lake
Gently massaged
By the waves
Content to let the current
Carry them where it may.

We have much to learn
From our feathered friends
Who surrender to the flow
From beginning to end.

TODAY: Are you always racing around trying to get things done in double-quick time so that you can move onto the next thing? Do obstacles always rear their head as if the universe were against you somehow? We convince ourselves that if we can control all aspects of our lives (and those around us) that all will be well, but it doesn't work out that way. We end up exhausted, stressed and anxious. Could it be that it's *you* who is moving against the rhythm of the universe?

Today, think of ways in which you can be like the ducks in the above poem, *i.e.* stop trying to fight the current and instead "surrender to the flow" of life. There is a great feeling of release and relief when you hand over this need to control.

This Love We Share

A kiss from you
And I'm melting
A caress from you
And the world disappears.
I trace the contours
Of your body in my mind
Linked together
In Divine blissful union.

The touch of your hand
Makes my heart sing.
The smell of you,
So familiar now.

I vow to you
From this day forth
To love and respect you
Honor and cherish you
Laugh and cry with you
Do it all with you.

So, kiss and caress me
Make me laugh,
Make me smile
And let the world disappear
Again for a while.

I wrote this poem to celebrate the marriage of two lovely friends whom I love very much. I was also mindful while I wrote it of my own marriage which has lasted 25 years, and I realized that the sentiments in the poem still rang true for me all these years later. So, today, if you find yourself taking your partner for granted, stop, rewind and instead tell them why you love and appreciate them!

Acts of Love and Kindness

Doesn't it feel great when we are on the receiving end of an act of kindness: the door held open for us; the cup of tea in bed; the prayer said on our behalf! And, you know, it feels *even better* to do an act of kindness for someone else, and not expect any praise or thanks in return.

TODAY, here are some simple acts of kindness you can do for others:

- hold the door open for them;
- make them a cup of tea or coffee;
- say a prayer for someone in need;
- write a positive review on social media of their business/ service;
- send them a card to show them that you're thinking of them;
- thank them when they do an act of kindness for you!

Make up your own "acts of kindness list" and try to do one each day. Do all these things simply because it feels like the kind thing to do. Be careful of your motivation though. If you find yourself feeling a little annoyed because the person didn't thank you, that's your ego wanting praise. This makes the act all about *you* and not them, and therefore detracts greatly from the act of kindness itself. It doesn't matter whether they thank you or not. All that matters is that you do something selfless for someone else.

The Storm's Coming

Warm Sahara air billows its way from the south
Snaking a path through the thermals
Gently, Insistently, nudging life on.

Crickets message to announce the approaching storm
Grasses bristle and crackle, gasping for air.
The storm's coming.

Timber shutters slap with annoyance. Thirsty. Dry.
The sensual coiling of the flagpole chain
Chinks rhythmically with the quickening
Heartbeat of the wind.
The storm's coming.

I sit at the window watching clouds march closer
Like a cohort on patrol
Taking no prisoners, no giving way.

Is there a greater spectacle
Than the approaching storm?
That freeze-frame of energy
Between scenes,
As nature's stagehands
Dismantle one view
And sketch out the next
In glorious sensory pleasure
… It's here!

Gossamer Wings and Squeals of Delight

One summer's morning, I was doing my usual short walk with the dogs in the field opposite our home. The grasses were growing almost to knee height and hummed with the sounds of bumble bees, crickets and flies. The sky was the clearest of blue and the sun's rays gently warmed my bones. It was such a beautiful day! As we walked, I looked across the field and saw a perfect circle of blue flowers and my immediate thought was, "Oh, it's like a fairy ring." As soon as I said this, the first two lines of the following poem flooded into my mind, so quickly that I had to keep repeating them over and over lest I forget them ("Faerie rings where nature sings its joyful call to play. Faerie rings where nature sings its joyful call to play" … and then the next line went something like, "Sandalphon's strings ring out within …"). "Who is Sandalphon?" I asked myself as I rushed the dogs back home so that I could write down the rest of the poem which was dancing into my head and conveying the whole magical scene. What a joy! The poem has a child-like rhythm to it. You can just imagine fairies or children skipping around as they chant it! PS. I had to look up who Sandalphon is. He is an Archangel (some say he was the prophet Elijah on Earth). He is reputed to be a protector of the Earth and is strongly associated with heavenly celestial music. Whether you believe this or not, try to find time to engage your inner child today.

> Faerie rings
> Where nature sings
> Its joyful call to play.
> Sandalphon's strings
> Ring out within
> This woodland sphere of blue.
>
> Nymphs and sprites

And flames so bright
Frolic and spin
Alive in the night.

Gossamer wings
Flit to and fro
And squeals of delight
Permeate the site.

This sacred sphere,
This magical sight
The woods are alive
With Faeries tonight!

The Bothy: a short story

PART TWO: Adam

"Jim!" He heard the cry and spun around to see who was shouting him. Apart from a few rustles from the denuded trees, he could hear nothing, although his ears strained as he leant into the direction it had come from.

"How odd," thought Jim. "Must have been the buzzard." His internal voice spoke up, suggesting he go into the Bothy and warm himself through at the fire. "Good idea," mumbled Jim. His face was so numb now he could scarcely feel it.

"Hey! I thought I heard somebody out there." The outstretched hand and broad smile greeted Jim like an old friend and he leant in to shake the younger man's hand.

"Hello. I'm glad to see you've got a fire burning. It's so cold out here," said Jim as he slipped his backpack from his shoulders and let it fall to the ground. A few flakes of snow fell from his head as he scanned the interior in the dim light. The smell was the first thing to assault the senses. You could almost taste the memories of log fires, tobacco and shared whisky which seemed to permeate the walls like distant echoes. There were two bunks, a simple table with two chairs which didn't match, and the fireplace complete with an iron pot or kettle. Most of all it felt warm and welcoming.

"It has everything you need doesn't it?" The younger man was holding the door ajar and he turned to look at Jim with an inquisitive expression creasing his forehead and eyes twinkling briefly.

"Oh, yes. It looks wonderful actually," Jim stammered. He took off his jacket and scarf, now encrusted with slivers of ice, and crossed the threshold into the warm interior.

"Come and warm up at the fire. I had a feeling I'd be getting company today. Here." A warm mug of milky tea was placed into Jim's hand by the generous stranger.

As he held the mug in both hands relishing the warmth, Jim considered his host. He'd say he was mid-thirties, a handsome lad, although his hair was too long for Jim's liking. Most of all though, he was easy to talk to and put him at his ease straight away. That was a skill Jim would love to possess, but he was way too nervous and jumpy in company, always trying too hard to please, so that people would enjoy themselves. Yet the harder he tried, the more anxious he would become and his jagged energy seemed to infect everyone else in the room, with the result that no one appeared to be enjoying themselves.

"I'm Jim. Nice to meet you, and thanks for this." Jim raised the mug of tea to his mouth as if offering a toast.

"Jim. Good to meet you. I'm Adam. What are you doing out here, man?"

"Huh? Oh, well I came to find myself, funnily enough," Jim replied, almost by way of an apology. He stifled a nervous laugh and shuffled in his seat by the fire to await the ridicule which was sure to follow.

"Find yourself, eh?" Adam leant back in his chair, brushing his long hair away from his face. "Well, you've come to the right place, Jim." (… to be continued.)

Thunderous Land

Like a snarling, seething
Wolf she comes
Enraged and belligerent
With one sole aim:
To clear the decks.

Her talons of fury
Shredding the
Decay of inertia
And licking at the
Wounds of torpor.

What a display is this
Of Divine creation!
Terrestrial elements
In re-orchestration
Then, finally sated,
Abating.

Leaving freshness and newness
Unimaginable brightness.
Our world is refreshed
And the she-wolf can rest.

Liberty

In my dream world
I see animals roam free
Not peered at through
The bars of a cage.

The scent of liberty
Carries thick in the air
Like the heady perfume
Of hibiscus blooms.

I see wisdom and compassion
Flow in men
Like a river of hope,
Returning these souls
From whence they came.

Sweet nectar of innocence
The shared gain.

The longing for home
Grows swiftly.
Captivity
A forgotten cruelty.

In my dream world
All are free
To fulfil their own destiny.

Spiritual Qualities: Purity of Heart

Blessed are the pure in heart: for they shall see God.
Matthew 5:8

There have been many great saints and masters (e.g. Jesus, Krishna, Mahatma Gandhi, Paramahansa Yogananda, Saint Francis etc.) who have come to Earth to show us how we can be better, kinder human beings, in order for our souls to grow and become closer to God. Saints are pure in heart; pure in thoughts, words and deeds. That's an enormous example for us to follow, but if we take one desirable spiritual quality at a time and work on nurturing that within us, before moving on to the next, we will get there! Fear not.

What is purity of heart?
Purity of heart for me conjures up the idea of thinking of and putting others above ourselves—always—with no selfish motives on our part of seeking either praise or thanks. That's tough isn't it? Try doing this for just one minute at a time, then for an hour, then try and incorporate it into your day. When I wake up in the morning, I ask: "Okay, God, how can I be kind today?" and I actively look out for opportunities during the day to do something kind for someone else. It's about entraining ourselves with new, positive habits and ways of thinking and being. It will eventually become automatic. It's not easy, but that's the point. God isn't going to give away his gifts to a half-hearted aspirant!

Some easy ways to nurture purity of heart in your day:
- Don't overthink things. If it feels right to do something for someone, do it!
- Do something you don't enjoy and do it gladly!
- Be grateful for the simple blessings in your life (a warm, safe

home; food on the table; being born into a lovely family and so on).

- Be mindful of the motivations behind your "selfless" acts. (Are you even *subconsciously* seeking praise, attention or thanks?)
- Don't allow yourself to be swayed emotionally by events (in other words, try to be even-minded, not over-excitable nor overly upset). This is like a cleansing routine for the heart, keeping it pure.
- Think of God often. Put your trust in Him.
- Maintain positivity in your thoughts. Thoughts are so powerful and can lead us down the shaky path of negativity and mistrust if we let them. Don't! Keep your mind, as well as your heart, pure!

Puff! Puff! Puff!

Dandelion seeds
Detach from the parent
Blown by the wind
To settle where they can.

Divine sparks of life
Dispersing and dividing
To populate these lands

To make a new life,
Ignorant of Source
And the filaments of connection
Still trailing in their wake.

Puff! And they're set free
On the adventure that is life

Puff! Growing strong now
Being the best that they can

Puff! A final surrender of self
So that offspring may thrive.

Flex

Flex like the beech tree
On a warm summer's day
Her cool, verdant canopy
Inhales the sun's rays

Her branches offer shelter
And a home for the needy
While creatures big and small
Are sustained by her bounty

Her trunk is a leaning post
For lovers' embraces
Her stature belies
The sweetest of natures

She delights in each challenge
Sister Weather sends her way:

Rain—a wonderful drink after
A thirsty day!
Wind—a gleeful opportunity to play!
Storm—"Let's see what we're made of"
She cries,

"For my strength lies
Not in my size
But in my capacity to flex."

Sentinels

Pure white sands and turquoise blue waters
Frame the Sentinels' view
Tall and strong they stand
These robust endeavors of the faithful.

A harsh land this where no tree
Survives, peat bogs their only terrain
The Stones have seen lives born
And torn apart by strife
Lovers entwined in their shadows
Widows mourning in sorrow.

The blueprint of the past lies
Embedded in their skin
An energetic imprint for future kin.

They feel cold to the touch, like ice
But a fiery heart lies within
A gift from the ancestors
Our eternal protectors
Sheltering us from the wild Atlantic winds.

This poem was inspired by the Prehistoric Standing Stones on the Isle of Lewis (Scotland), which are a firm testament to the steadfastness and resilience of those who labored to erect them. This Midsummer they remind us to stand firm to our beliefs, show resilience and keep on keeping on.

The Ultimate Staycation

(Article first published in *InterAction for M.E.* magazine, Issue: Summer 2018)

You may not be able to travel, but with a little imagination and willpower, you can still give yourself a break. It's been ten years since I've physically been able to go on holiday due to severe M.E. and Fibromyalgia, which have left me virtually housebound. However, by using my willpower and imagination, I've succeeded in taking many stress-free, alternative summer holidays—and so can you. Here are my top tips for the ultimate staycation:

1. Take a "visualization excursion." Look through some photographs of a favorite holiday from the past. Then, sitting or lying down with eyes closed, bring to mind the sights, sounds, smells, places you visited and who you went with. Remember a particularly relaxing and happy day and how it made you feel. Don't look back with melancholy, but rather with gratitude and contentment. Immerse yourself in this relaxing mental excursion for as long as you like, but at least a few minutes so that your heart and pulse rate slow and positive emotions are given space to flood your system with natural endorphins.

2. Transport yourself to a different world with a book. Choose a book set in the destination that you love (fiction or non-fiction book, whichever you prefer). If you can't read a physical book due to muscle fatigue, try an e-book or audio book. I tend to choose books with short chapters and not too many characters as concentration and memory can be problematic with M.E.

3. Journey abroad via the medium of film and TV. There are so

many options to choose from—programs on cookery, travel, documentaries, dramas, as well as movies set in your country of choice.

4. Take your taste buds on tour by eating the food of the country. If you are able, ask someone to take you out for a meal at an authentic restaurant (lunch is usually quicker and less stressful for those who are sensitive to light and noise). If you are not able to leave the house, many supermarkets do home deliveries, or you can order a takeaway. Eat outside if you can; feel the warmth of the sun's rays on your body and imagine yourself in your holiday destination.

5. Immerse yourself in the language and music of the country. Search online for podcasts that will teach you some phrases of the language you are interested in. This can be a lot of fun! Research singers and groups from your holiday country and download some authentic music to listen to.

For those of you who like to be organized (like me), you can even draw up an itinerary! Here's an example of what your holiday *could* look like:

	MORNING	AFTERNOON	EVENING
Monday	"Arrive." Sit outside if you can to read. Take a selfie and post on social media.	Watch a film or documentary on travel, art or cookery. Siesta.	Go out to a restaurant or prepare an authentic meal at home.
Tuesday	Eat an authentic breakfast. Take a visualization excursion.	Do a language podcast.	Watch a film set in your holiday destination. Have authentic drinks and snacks.

	MORNING	AFTERNOON	EVENING
Wednesday	Use an online site such as *canva.com* to create and send holiday postcards. This is easy and fun and you will be learning new skills!	Share on your social media page. Siesta. Read a holiday book or watch a movie set in country. Siesta.	Order authentic takeaway food. Write a journal of your holiday activities so far.
Thursday	Sit outside and research a little of the history of the country while listening to its music.	Buy little gifts (online) to give to friends and family as a memento of your holiday.	"Depart." Do a visualization exercise to recall all that you have done on your holiday!

Wherever you "go" on holiday this year, I do hope you enjoy yourself—and remember, the only limitations are your imagination and willpower!

Samadhi: Ecstasy

Lying here in the arms of my love
Replete, content, safe.
The afternoon sun meanders
Through the drapes
As we bask in the afterglow
Of beautiful union.

I give thanks to You Lord
In this sacred moment.
For just as this man cares gently
For my body, so do You also
Nourish my Soul.

Calling me to You in so many ways
Sharing Your joy when I answer
Holding me close in Your tender embrace.
Enabling me to surrender.

I am happy in this moment
I am content in this life
Till ultimate reunion with You
In Ecstasy: Samadhi.

Reflections of God

The Lord lives in the hearts of all beings.
– The Bhagavad Gita, 18:61

To believe that we are all made in the image of God is to understand that we are all created equally on Earth. This means that when we judge another, we judge the part of ourselves that is reflected in that person. This could be an aspect of ourselves that we need to change. Every action we take affects all others because we are so interconnected. I like to think of the world as a tapestry with all life on earth forming the disparate threads which knit it together to make the whole. If the threads didn't knit strongly together, the tapestry would be weak.

TODAY: Remember that love is the key that holds us all together in peace and harmony and love resides in our hearts. If our hearts are closed off, we can't be open to receiving or giving love. My heart was closed off for a long time until a certain blonde cute little girl came into my life and wedged herself firmly into my heart where she has remained to this day. I hadn't realized I was so closed off until I felt the overwhelming waves of love for this little soul as she looked up at me from my lap. She is called Amber and she is my dog. Love comes to us in all shapes and sizes. It can even seem harsh at first, like someone telling us off for our bad behavior (this *is* an act of loving kindness if you think about it!). We simply need to be ready to receive love in whatever form it takes, and to reciprocate!!!

The Meadow

Meadow-sweet grasses
Trampled underfoot
Releasing herbal scent-pods
To swirl in our midst.

Summer heat rising:
Shimmering nebula
Of movement and sound
A symphonic concerto
Playing in my mind.

Seed pods acquiesce
Their progeny dispersed
By the languid breeze.

The world is at ease
On this Midsummer's Eve.
And the meadow shares
Her beauty with all.

Cosmic Song

The feelings for this poem built up over a couple of days. I had been listening to some wonderful music by Deva Premal, and the track *Om Mantra (The Cosmic Yes)* was resonating so strongly with me. My whole body was buzzing in a sort of recognition. I could quite strongly see myself on a rooftop in an Indian city, sitting awaiting the arrival of the dawn, listening to the sounds of the city thrumming like the cosmic Om. As I meditated last night, the words for the poem came into my mind. I hope you enjoy it.

Sitting on a rooftop
On this steamy summer's morn
30°C: Awaiting the dawn.

The distant hum of city life
Builds and thrums
In time with my pulse
Like distant drums.

I hear the sounds of life
Becoming louder,
Coming nearer; humming
The tune of the Creator.

This Cosmic Song
In praise of the Sun
Resonant harmony
Of the One.

The strains of a sitar
Carry in the air
As I sit and stare

At this glorious scene
Unfolding before me:
A Cosmic dream.

My life is this life
Here and everywhere.
This rooftop my armchair
A magical transporter
To the inner realm of peace.

I sing the song of my heart
In unison with the Sun
As it spreads its joyous light
Over each and everyone.
A-um... A-um... A-um...

▶ *Watch the YouTube video poem.*

Carriages at Dawn

Moonlight glistens on tiny crystals
Dancing hypnotically on wispy dresses
Laughter sprinkles its infectious fun
In the giggles of children darting around
Squealing like piglets separated from Mum.
Flowers in hair, confetti in the air
Soft kisses stolen in the night
Eyes shine bright
As whoops of delight
Carry from the dance floor.
One song over
Then shouts for "More!"
Aunts and uncles crumple onto chairs
Cheeks flushed, brows mopped
Smiling joyful tears
At the exertion of muscles
Little used in recent years.
Cake cut, photos snapped
The tempo is relaxed
As shoulders stifle rising yawns…
The celebration continues
Till Carriages at Dawn.

Refuge of Solace

I have episodes of anxiety and depression. I liken it to "falling down a well". Usually I can get on with my daily life, although the well is always in the peripheral of my vision. Sometimes, though, I find myself at the bottom of the well. This can be a scary, lonely place where the mind is full of fear: "Will I manage to get back out?" I know now that of course I will, for every low mood or depression will pass like storm clouds, leaving me refreshed and renewed.

So, instead of viewing the well as a prison, I see it as a temporary refuge of solace, a quiet place of safety which allows me to ride out the storm. If you are affected by anxiety or depression, find a safe place in your mind, use distraction techniques and ask people for help. Much love.

I sit by the well
Enjoying the shade
On this hot summer's day in July.
I hear its liquid contents
Drip to the pool at the base;
The base with the seat
Inscribed with my name.
For this is my domain
When I fall down the well:
The place where depression dwells.
I can see the clouds above
And the sun peeking through behind
And I know that this too shall pass:
It's just a storm in my mind.
So, I distract myself—
Counting bricks and all my blessings,
Finding faces among the mosses
Which cling to this temporary home:

My refuge of solace
Till the storm clouds move on.

The Flowers are Singing

The title for this poem arose from a character in a television drama (*Versailles*), at the point of her death, saying that she could hear the flowers singing. I thought this was such a beautiful, comforting image, and so this poem took shape. If we can suspend belief in the Universe being all there is and our body-mind being all we are, then the other realm after death becomes a magical place of wonder and joy. I no longer fear death, which is a wonderful gift in itself, because I long to return to Spirit when my time comes.

Slow, like the breeze
On a hot summer's eve,
Billowing their beauty for us all to see.
Roses and lavenders,
Heady perfumiers
The flowers are singing
In this realm of make-believe.

Their joyous refrain
Bides us sweetly to their domain
Of love, of tenderness and peace.
Their floral charms
Soothe and disarm us
To venture, untethered,
From pain to release.

I long to hear the flowers sing
And feel their perfume
Uplifting my soul
And carrying me home.

I long to join their floral song
In a choral crescendo of love.
I long to belong.

Slow, like the breeze
On a hot summer's eve,
The flowers are singing
In this realm of make-believe.

The Divine Goddess:
Healing our planet through compassion

(previously published in *The Divine Goddess: When She Rules*, Golden Dragonfly Press, 2017)

It was to my earthly mother that I ran when I cut myself as a child. She would comfort me in her arms, cleanse the wound then apply a healing salve before sending me out again into the world—renewed, rejuvenated, uplifted. It is to my spiritual Mother that I turn again and again for all of life's challenges. She resides in my inner wisdom, in my growing intuition, in a longing to show love and kindness to all life. She is known by many titles, such as Divine Goddess, Sacred Feminine, Moon Goddess, Divine Mother among others. I watch her influence smooth its healing balm across the planet, knitting together our self-inflicted wounds of egotism, intolerance, judgement and ignorance. I see her reflection in each full moon simultaneously pulling me skyward and inward. I feel her energy course through me during meditation, writing and periods of reflection or prayer. I hear her matter-of-fact voice answering my questions with the tolerance and patience of a heart full of love.

The spirit of the Goddess permeates all life on Earth. Her call can be heard in the ether as she re-exerts herself in a rebalancing of planetary energies. Sometimes she whispers a gentle lullaby on the breeze; at others, her rage carves through the air like a fierce harridan: dispersing old energy to make way for the new. I believe we need a state of balance in our lives—mental, physical, spiritual and emotional—for us to thrive. The Goddess energy has been growing in recent months and years to counterbalance the ego-bound mores of intolerance, distrust and fear which have pervaded our dealings with each other over the centuries. More and more, we awaken to what is needed now: a raising of the vibration of love and compassion in all our hearts. A beautiful consequence of this inner healing journey to re-balance ourselves is that we are then better equipped to spread love and kindness to those around us. We can lead by example not judgement; we can be guided by intuition not fear; we can accept difference with delight not suspicion. This is the Goddess in action!

I perceive the Divine Feminine slowly yet firmly infiltrating the establishments of power on Earth, and with this soft invasion comes a turnaround in business and politics, proffering new, positive ways of working together. These are not evident at first glance. A level of discernment is needed to stop and evaluate what we see and hear. Let's actively seek out these pearls of grace which encircle the planet yet have for so long been obscured by our ingrained habits of ignorance and desire. Below are some of the Goddess pearls which brighten our lives. As kindred spirits and carriers of the light, we ought to make it our sacred duty to share this divine Goddess energy with others:

- The rise in social enterprises; not-for-profit companies; and cooperatives, often employing those whom society has traditionally shunned, such as the homeless, ex-criminals, long-term unemployed etc. Profits ploughed back into the future well-being of the company, employees, local area and charitable causes; everyone paid a wage affording them a decent standard of living. Social enterprises imbue a sense of purpose in their employees, awakening in them a willingness to serve others for the good of all, to work not solely for individual personal gain but also collectively contributing to society as a whole. These are true examples of the Divine Feminine energies of compassion, intuitive wisdom and understanding merging with business acumen for the profit of all. My hope is that we will frequent these enterprises in our local areas, helping them to flourish.

- The rise in positive journalism coupled with new university courses fit for the 21st century—such as Holistic science, Ecology and spirituality and Sustainable horticulture. These are further examples of the Sacred Feminine energies continuing to restore balance to all areas of society. The old norms in the media and education sectors are being worn down as intolerance cedes to a growing level of compassion and understanding among the populace.

- Women assuming a valued place on company boards and in politics, enabling a re-balancing of decision-making at the top levels in society and often leading by example in new ways of cooperative governance. We only need to look at the rising number of powerful female world leaders in countries such as Germany, Croatia, Switzerland, UK, Malta and many more, to see the Goddess energy evolving and changing our world, ushering in a new paradigm of peaceful resolution to conflict.

- The resurgence of crafts and the traditional ways of doing things. The "old" (feminine) wisdom of healing herbs, of make-do and mend, of making our clothes and growing our own food—these have all recently made the transition to mainstream institutions, homes and new businesses after half a century of being consigned to the peripheries. Society now values these creative skills and attributes.

Finally, one truly powerful way in which I encounter the Goddess energy vibration is in meditation. I experience Her love as a blossoming in the heart chakra, once closed off through sorrow, fear and negativity, but now infused with ever-new joy, contentment and positivity. I feel the tendrils of the Divine Mother reach out across my chest and upwards to connect with the higher chakras, like the sweetest-smelling clematis climbing ever skyward towards the life-giving Universal light. Old habits and blockages are dissolved in the nectar of Her love. She is forgiving, understanding, kind and compassionate. She imbues me with her wisdom and love for all that is—seen and unseen. She is my saving grace! Let us embrace this Goddess energy in every cell of our being by following our inner wisdom, listening to our growing intuition, and showing love and kindness to all life—for that is the legacy of the Sacred Feminine.

In the Flow

Time stands still in the flow
Slow-motion ecstasy of Being
At one with the ease of Doing.
Gliding through waters of calm
Alive in the moment.
Breath of life swirling around
A cocoon of peace suspended in situ.
The past has no future here
Only the present remains
Reaching out to Infinity
In a longing embrace.

Step off the Roller-Coaster

Loved ones watch from a distance
This man-made spectacle of fun.
Their necks craned in anticipatory glee
Connected somehow, sharing each emotion:
The fear of the ascent as the car inches higher
Breathless, hearts pumping.
Then plummeting terror as mortality beckons
A venal injection like no other.

They observe it all, clapping and cheering
Amidst gasps and cries.
For there is no up without down
Fear cannot exist without love
You need to step on to step off.

Have we tasted all of God's gifts
And found them wanting?
Still we want more, so we create our own:
Bigger, faster, more extreme.
Our pleasures know no limits.

But this virtual world-within-a-world
Is only an illusory reflection
In an endless hall of mirrors.
Step off the roller-coaster to find peace.
Please others to please yourself.
Come back to God.
He's been watching and waiting too!

How May I Serve?

As I sit and ponder this wonderful Earth
I ask myself: *How May I Serve?*
I seek not glory nor wealth beyond my needs
I ask not for beauty or possessions
For a temple built on these is weak
And sure to crumble.

What is my role in Your paradise here?
To find myself again
To seek You everywhere
To radiate this peace in my heart to the world
To heal with my thoughts
And comfort with my words.

May everything I think, say and do
This day be in service of You.

TODAY: Remember, everyone can serve. We each have a role to play on God's Earth. Simply be yourself, meditate each day and your true purpose will be revealed to you.

Remember to put the glass down!

This is a story my brother John relayed to me when I was sharing with him one day about how stressed I was feeling. The story appeared on reddit.com but I could not find anyone to attribute it to, so I thank the Universe for bringing it to my and your attention. Here it is:

A psychologist walked around a room while teaching stress management to an audience. As she raised a glass of water, everyone expected they'd be asked the "half empty or half full" question. Instead, with a smile on her face, she inquired: "How heavy is this glass of water?"

Answers called out ranging from 8oz to 20oz.

She replied, "The absolute weight doesn't matter. It depends on how long I hold it. If I hold it for a minute, it's not a problem. If I hold it for an hour, I'll have an ache in my arm. If I hold it for a day, my arm will feel numb and paralyzed. In each case, the weight of the glass doesn't change, but the longer I hold it, the heavier it becomes."

She continued, "The stresses and worries in life are like that glass of water. Think about them for a while and nothing happens. Think about them a bit longer and they begin to hurt. And if you think about them all day long, you will feel paralyzed— incapable of doing anything."

Remember to put the glass down.

Little Ripples

I believe we are all interconnected on Earth. Everything we think, say and do affects all others, if not in this life, then in the next. Here are two things to focus on today to strengthen our interconnectedness:

1. Treat people with respect, how you would like to be treated.
2. Stop trying to fight the current. You can never control it! Life is so much easier and more loving when you accept this and go with the flow.

> Little ripples,
> Delicate rays on the
> Vast ocean of thought
> And energy;
> At one with the other
> In sublime synergy;
> Ebbing and flowing
> With the passage of time.
>
> I shall float on this ocean
> For eternity
> And carry its sigh
> Through my bones;
> Feel its gentle bliss
> Like a silken kiss
> Up my spine;
> Surrender to its will
> As my soul basks in joy.
>
> I shall glide
> Through these waters
> Untroubled by waves

Of emotion;
In tune with the current
Of Cosmic bliss;
This languid embrace
My home shall be
From now till Eternity.

I shall sail
Through this ocean
Singing its harmony
Vibrating its potency;
Flowing, acquiescing,
to the Creator's love.
I am a happy, little ripple
On my way home!

We are One

This poem came to me after reading about violence at a football (soccer) match. Now this is not unusual in the UK (especially in Scotland, where we have the added "bonus" of overindulgence in alcohol and religious sectarianism between rival teams). It's quite an atrocious and depressing, seemingly never-ending story which has been ever thus. Well, perhaps we can't change the past, BUT we can change how things are now and in the future. How? In the following ways:

- by changing how we think about them;
- by modifying our exposure to negative, hype-filled news stories;
- by changing how we allow these stories to affect us;
- by changing how we talk about them (especially to our children);
- by changing our actions (positive words of encouragement to the younger generation are all and good but pointless without your modified actions to back these up!).

Memories of competition slide
Under an avalanche of hate
Blanketing soul understanding
Swelling the ego's pride.
But what price a rival's *pate*?

Differences in perception yield
Over-spilling the playing field
With hatred's flash fury
Cheered on with delight
Like an unexpected penalty
In a goal-less night.

A behemoth of rage
All snarling teeth
And hackles raised
Stampedes through the stadium
Now shattered to the core
Where ashes lie smoldering
In endless uproar.

This spectacle our focus
Till close of doors.
When we re-frame our vision
And surrender once more
To love's healing light.

Memories of hatred subside
Cleansed by evening rain
Erasing judgement's stain
When calming heartbeats
Invite compassion
Once more to reign
And the body, mind and soul
Join together again.

TODAY: Remember that the sun doesn't differentiate upon whom it shines its rays, and rain falls from the sky for everyone. So why should we withhold our gifts and blessings from those whom we feel are different? Sharing our love, kindness and understanding with others from whom we feel "separate" or different (rather than solely with our family and friends) is a much more difficult, yet worthwhile, spiritual task!

Flame of Ignition

Gratitude grows
And envelops the world
Like frosting on a cake
To be savored with love.

The body is nourished
With the bread of life
The soul is replenished
With Your Everlasting light.

For this is Your body
This is Your mind
You are in every place and time.

Flame of Ignition
The eternal fire within
Never extinguished
Though often diminished
By our ignorant will.

Yet You welcome us in
When we knock at the door
Pulling back the curtain
To discover You there.

God the Creator
Great Source of cognition
May Your breath
Fan the flames of our
Acceptance and love
A gift to our hearts
From Your realm above.

Autumn

Introduction to Autumn:

Autumn, or Fall. Where do I begin to describe my love for this wonderful season? This is a time of abundance, of reaping the rewards for all our efforts in earlier seasons. It bristles with symbolic parallels of the seasons of our life (and indeed seasons referring to successive lifetimes on earth). In recent decades, especially in the West, our connection with the land had diminished to such a degree that the majority no longer understood the traditional importance of the harvest: to farmers, communities and nations. I have a distant memory from childhood of there being extended "working holidays" during this time to allow truckloads of men to harvest potatoes and other crops, for much of it was still done by hand (in the 1960s–1970s) before the onset of major mechanization.

This shared experience of the harvest engendered a sense of community and gave local residents a degree of "ownership" of the harvest. As nations, we rely on the land to feed our peoples—the fertile areas are referred to as "the breadbasket" and so on. A successful harvest has always traditionally ensured plenty of food to sustain us over the winter.

There are still many countries in the world where their peoples retain this deep connection with the land, knowing instinctively the optimum time to harvest, neighbor helping neighbor, guided by the moon. In the West in recent years, there has been a welcome resurgence and interest in "going back to our roots", that is to say of growing our own food, and eating locally-sourced food (and you will have read more on this in the Goddess essay which was included in the section on Summer). In my eyes, this is evidence of the cycle of connection with the land beginning anew: our ancestors lived off the land [birth and preservation]; as we became industrialized (and in our veiled eyes, more "civilized"), land became a commodity, food was wasted and the resources of the land were no longer shared fairly [this is the decay and death part of the cycle of eternal life]. Now we are returning to the birth section of the cycle. This is evidenced by the proliferation of food banks to share surplus food with the needy, as well as a huge reduction in food waste (which is now being used for biomass heating systems, using up leftovers, sharing surplus food with others via community fridges and cafes and so on).

Autumn is also the time for harvest festivals, I suppose the most famous being Thanksgiving in the USA, but harvest festivals are also celebrated in many churches to thank God for all the gifts he has given us. The symbolism of the natural world is at its height in Autumn: we have the Harvest Moon, which tends to be bigger and brighter. This is the full moon which falls closest to the autumn equinox and it was called harvest moon because in the past before the advent of electricity, this moon extended the light to enable farmers a longer time to harvest their crops. We also have the symbolism and importance of women as personifications of Mother Earth—the givers of life around this time. I particularly love the symbolism of the seed which contains the essence of eternal life. This is evident in plants but also resides hidden within us.

I often rise before dawn and have the secret pleasure of watching day break over the meadow across from my home. Secret because I'm up before anyone else in the household, and it feels that the pleasure of this dawn is meant for me alone! There's nothing quite like an Autumn morning: light wisps of mist or heavier swathes of fog seem to form a protective layer over all life "under the dome". As I watch the change of the guard in the colors of the sky from pinks to blues, my spirits are lifted along with the mist and negative thoughts soon evaporate into the ether. This is a timeless, wondrous beauty that seems to pause life in a freeze-frame of energy allowing the senses full access.

Autumn is indeed my favorite season of the year. As leaves

change color and draw their life-energy inwards, so I believe it is with our spiritual journey to discover our Divine beauty within. Having spent many years meditating with my devotional meditation group (we follow the teachings and example set by our Guru, Sri Paramahansa Yogananda), I know the benefits of interiorization, of pulling the senses inwards in order to calm the mind of restless thoughts. This calm mind, this stillness, allows us to reconnect with our inner divinity. It seems to me that this is what the natural world is doing too at this time: withdrawing its life energy in preparation for a period of repose, of building up inner reserves and holding these in stasis over winter, before the cycle of growth begins again in spring.

There is a vulnerability in dropping all their leaves to reveal their true form underneath and yet they stand firm, unaffected. This is a stage through which man is required to pass if we want to progress spiritually. To do so, we need to be willing to subject ourselves to compassionate self-analysis and reform; identifying and discarding old habits of behavior which are based in fear, are negative and unhelpful to us and others, and replacing them with new, positive ways of thinking and being. I talk about this inner work in more depth in my book, *Acts of Kindness from Your Armchair* (Ayni Books, 2017). *This* is the "stripping away of our leaves" to reveal our true form underneath. It's scary because we fear others' disapproval of our true selves. Surely, we're not good enough just as we are? Well yes indeed, we are! More than good enough. We are amazing. We all come from God; we all have the God-spark within us. We're capable of so much more than we realize.

And just like the plants and trees, our bodies are constantly in a state of change. Our cells, our blood, our skin, our bones—all these things—are renewed many times as we go through life. Each day has a beginning, a middle and an end: birth, preservation and death, reflecting the rhythm and cycle apparent in all life on Earth. This solidifies in my mind the notion that we are all interconnected. Everything on earth is born, is maintained and dies; even our thoughts, our words, our emotions, our ideas. Everything and everyone on Earth is linked—each atom, each cell, each person. Thus, our thoughts, words and actions affect all life, including the animal and natural worlds.

These themes of stasis, renewal and interconnectedness run through the poems of this season. From "A Mother's Lament" (the pain of separation, parent from child); "This Time Around", which explores the themes of reincarnation and the very nature of what it means to give life to another; there are words of love and forgiveness; there are poems about sisterhood and finding God within. You will also see some verse of a more metaphysical nature about the true nature of reality and how this is hidden from man through "maya", as described in Hindu philosophy as the veil or screen of delusion which hides from us our true reality as immortal beings of spirit and not these finite corporeal frames that we inhabit for a short time. These are also my beliefs. This is my true nature "stripped bare".

A Mother's Lament

The following poem was inspired by a BBC television program about life on the remote Scottish island of Fair Isle (famous for knitwear!). As the island is so tiny, pupils are only taught up to the age of 11, after which time they then need to attend boarding school on the neighboring island of Shetland. The torment I witnessed on the faces of the parents was heartbreaking: having to be separated from their children at such an early age for weeks at a time. These lines try to convey the torment of the mother, whose inner child eventually cries out to her Father (God) to ease her pain. Hope you enjoy the poem.

> The boat to the isles
> ferries you away from me
> churning up foam in a carefree goodbye.
> Unlike I. Here I stand
> naked to the core
> half-drowning in emotions
> swelling up inside me.
> Jack-knifed by opposing currents
> of longing and letting go
> of holding on and setting free.
> How will you be on your return?
> will you race to my embrace
> all open-arms and giddiness?
> Still the child I recognize.
> Or will the weeks apart
> have steadied your heart?
> Given you sea legs to walk
> your own path.
> The foam-tossed waters
> sail you away from me.
> their precious cargo now

hidden from view.
I turn and return to my life left in stasis—
chickens to feed, ewes to shear,
land to tend, hours to spend
casting wistful glances at clocks
Hoping that time will somehow zoom
into fast-forward,
bringing you safely back to me.
Rasping shallow breaths come:
I'm panicking.
"I can't do this. It's too difficult.
It's too soon."
The separation so intense,
I'm breaking.
Disintegrating into disparate shards
then buffering endlessly,
somnambulant,
unable to reconfigure
this new life today.
I wrap both arms around my shattered core
and murmur tenderly, "One minute, one hour,
one day at a time."
The child in me screams a plaintiff cry
to be gathered up in comforting arms
nestled snugly against Your chest
alive to Your heartbeat
soothing my breath.
Tomorrow will be a better day.

▶ *Watch the video poem.*

This Time Around

I didn't have children in this lifetime and spent many lost years mourning and regretting this loss. But a new-found certainty in the belief of reincarnation washed the stain of this deep sorrow from my heart and I felt free, healed. It's quite comforting to think that I've been a parent many times in the past. I didn't need to learn that lesson this time around. For me, compassion for *all* life, including animals, including those disabled or suffering in some way, as well as non-judgement have been the major lessons for me in this life.

I do think donating my organs when I have no further need of them would be a lovely gift to leave to other people to help *them* live a fuller life. We take from others throughout our lives, don't we, so for me it is right and fitting that I should give something back when I am finished with this body.

TODAY: If this is of interest to you, do some research, have the conversation with your loved ones and sign up for organ donation!

I didn't give birth to new life
This time around
I had other challenges to face.
But know that when I discard
This earthly shell
I shall give life aplenty
In my passing.

If these eyes may give sight to another,
Then take them.
If this heart may beat in another,
So, have it.

If these kidneys may revitalize another,
Why wouldn't I?

For I have no need for these things now.
I'm going home...
To the wonderful realm of thought.
I'm going home...
To kaleidoscopic eternal bliss.
I'm going home...
To awaken from the sleep state of earthly life.

So, do not grieve for this body.
Look in the eyes of another
—I am there.
Feel the beating heart of another
—I am there.
See vitality spring forth in another
—I am there.

Be happy and share in my joy
For I *did* give birth to new life
This time around.

The Great Link

Atoms bumping and jostling
Spreading the spark of the Divine.
Cells mingling and melding
Dividing and uniting in time.

So stand we around the bonfire
Fingers linked and hearts entwined.
As flames crackle and spark
Burning all boundaries
Soldering each link.

Moonlight casts its net upon us
Holding us tight, keeping us safe.
Its silvery wisdom a buoyancy vest
As we praise the Creator for this beautiful Earth.

TODAY: Take a few moments to look around you at this amazing planet that provides for all our needs, and really give thanks for all its blessings!

Change

Whatever our circumstances, we all face change in our lives. None of us is the person we once were. This took me some time to realize. At first, when illness changes your life you can easily drown in self-pity and/or anger.

Watching a television program about the Invictus Games jolted me out of this state of inertia. The Invictus Games is a competition for those from the armed forces who have been wounded and disabled in battle and can no longer serve. The courage these athletes show to grasp this new purpose in their life is humbling and a lesson to each of us. You may have heard the old adage: "There is always someone worse off than you."

I've learned not to tether myself to an idealistic view of the past as this taints the present and blocks new possibilities for the future. I've finally accepted this new reality as a gift. Perhaps outwardly we appear broken but we can change our lives from the inside out!

I lost myself a few years back
I thought my job was who I was
—but it wasn't.
I thought my health was here to stay
—but it didn't.
I looked to others for my happiness
—but it wasn't there.
I was shuffling along in a bad dream
Tethered to the expectations of others
Trying to divide and sub-divide myself
Into smaller and smaller pieces
Of dwindling light.

Now I see that loss makes space for the new
And every challenge is a step along the way

To where we're supposed to be.
There are no what ifs and why me's.
Leave them in the past
Where they're meant to be.
I have found myself again, curled up
Snugly in the arms of the Divine
Where I have been all this time.

TODAY: We all have pain in our lives (physical, mental, emotional, spiritual). It is there to teach us something about ourselves if we grasp the opportunity! There is always good that comes out of bad. Always. We may not be aware of it until much later on, but the seed will have been planted, ready to sprout. It can be very difficult to remain positive through times of change, but that's exactly the point. It's *how we react* to life's challenges that is the making of us.

The healing power of water!

Bad habits:
I've been working on trying to change my bad habits recently. I listed them all (at least all the ones I could think of!) and gave them a score between 1–10, with 10 being the most annoying to other people. I enlisted the help of my husband with this task! Then beside each bad habit I wrote the opposite (positive) quality that I wanted to encourage within myself. Top of my list to change were Impatience and Irritability, which I decided to replace with Calmness and Understanding.

How was I going to accomplish this?
Water—especially its healing and restorative powers—has been running through my mind (excuse the pun!) when I think about bad habits. I was thinking that we use water to cleanse our body of all sorts of toxins: we sweat, we urinate, we clean our teeth, we wash our hands, we take a shower, we wash clothes, we drink to hydrate ourselves and so on. And so, I decided that if we use water in this way to cleanse ourselves in the physical body, why not use its power to cleanse ourselves spiritually?

Here's how I do it:
Each time I come into contact with water throughout the day, I say my cleansing affirmation or mantra:

> *I release this bad habit of impatience/irritability. I don't want it anymore in my life. Please cleanse me of this habit; flush it away with the water and replace it with calmness/understanding.*

I say this when I wash my hands, when I pee, when I brush my teeth, when I step in a puddle, when I go out for a walk in the rain—any time I come into contact with water during the day. It's really refreshing actually and it does work. What you are doing is training the mind with a new, positive habit. This needs repetition, repetition, repetition for the habit to be ingrained! As I'm doing this, I'm also imagining what it feels like to experience the new, positive quality in its place.

Over to you!

TODAY: Why not give this a try?

Birdsong Greeting the Dusk

One evening I went out to sit in the garden just to take a few moments to relax, breathe in the intoxicatingly fragrant, evening air and drink my tea. Soon after I had settled myself on my garden bench, the birdsong began. It seemed to come from every tree and shrub in our garden (though I couldn't see any birds), our neighbors' gardens and from the more distant trees in the field opposite. The chattering "roll-call" quickly transformed into a beguiling symphony of different birds performing their parts, the most beautiful of all being that of the blackbird which, I'm sure, could enchant the hardest of hearts. Here is the poem I wrote as I sat in witness to this amazing spectacle of nature.

> The birdsong in my garden
> Is greeting the dusk
> This melody of sound
> Is circling around me
> Infusing my veins
> With a cleansing refrain.
>
> Vibratory salve,
> Mending all wounds
> Of sadness and regret
> Offering up blessings
> In each wave of sound.
>
> A healing crescendo
> Charges the air
> Then silence descends
> As nightfall's cooling net
> Swathes the land in peace.

The Flame of Transformation

Let the petals fall away
From the lotus blossom
That you are
See the eternal flame
Which lies at its heart

Gaze as the flame
Transforms into ribbons
Twirling their ascension
In psychedelic fission

Delight in the joy
Of Divine transformation
Offer yourself
As a conduit for God
To pour His light through
This vessel on Earth

Soar in the certainty
Of love from above
Before gentle re-entry
And spiritual rebirth.

This poem is about the process in yoga practice (as *I* experience it) of bringing the life energy up through the chakras in the spine to reach the center of Christ Consciousness between the eyebrows. The purpose of this is to bring us closer to God.

TODAY: Think of some things that you can do to bring yourself closer to God. It could be maintaining a cheerful attitude even if you are having a tough day; perhaps you could be extra kind to someone who is bad-tempered; maybe you could give up some of your time to visit a friend or relative in person.

Searing the Link

It can be so easy to succumb to the experience of pain, especially chronic pain. But if you believe that this body is not who we really are, that we are in fact immortal Spirit living in a mortal body, then this belief helps to assuage the "trauma"—emotional and physical—brought about by the experience of pain. This doesn't happen overnight, but like any good habit, it takes time to embed. One way I distract myself in the immediacy of a bout of pain is by reciting a mental gratitude list of everything good in (my) life; another is to do one of my "Go To" activities:

- I'll write a brief letter to someone who is struggling. It could be to a child suffering from a serious illness (www. sendkidstheworld.com) or a note to a sick or lonely friend/ relative (I keep some notelets at home for just this purpose).
- I'll clean something in my home *mindfully*, not rushing, but simply concentrating on doing that one thing and thinking only of that.
- I'll pray for a particular group of people who are struggling at that time (perhaps refugees, children in poverty, those who have no regular access to food and water).

These activities immediately transport me into the other person's shoes, so that I no longer think about my own worries. It does work, immediately! These are quick and easy strategies to relieve pain in the short-term, but if you are mobile, and if you are drawn to it, why not get involved in some way with longer-term projects, ones that resonate with you (loneliness, mental health, abuse, chronic physical pain and so on)? When we build a habit of helping other people (selfless service), our focus changes from inward-looking and often self-pitying, to outward-acting and "others-compassionate". In short, we become nicer people: kinder, more even-tempered, calmer.

TODAY: Try different short-term strategies to alleviate pain, perhaps a distraction activity like the ones above, a meditation or prayer for others (you can meditate or say a short prayer at your desk at work unnoticed by others). It is important to do something that soothes the initial body-panic brought on by the pain, and also quietens the chattering ego-mind to allow you to reconnect with your inner silence, for it is there that pain will dissipate. And you know, the silence is *always* there. You *will* find it the more you are in stillness. And when you experience it, you will want to continue with it, for inner stillness calms the heart and muscles and brings about a state of wonderful peace in your body-mind. Thoughts still come and go but if you ignore them, peace will reign. This is a spiritual battle which you can win if you will yourself to persevere. Here's the poem I wrote about overcoming pain, "Searing the Link":

> Pain: a reminder from Source
> That we are not of the body,
> A knee-jerk reaction
> To living a lie.
> Yet peaceful surrender
> The aching soul shall free
> Like whispered longings
> Blown by the breeze.
>
> This challenge like no other:
> Chronic malaise
> To be suffered.
> An eternal winter's darkness
> At the core of our being
> May yet be overcome .
> Through Divine union.

The mind forms the link
Between body and pain
Darting between cells
In a cascading refrain
Of despair.
So, distract it, ignore it,
Resolutely overcome it.

Cast overboard all despair
Like a fisherman his net.
Revisit the stillness
Of twinkling starlight
Where the veil is stretched thin
Between night and day,
Love and pain.

We originate from Source
A pain-free domain.
Divine power ignites
Our inner flame.

Know this and use this
To diffuse every cell
With His light,
Healing and numbing
The mind of its delusion,
Searing the link
With the flame of truth.

Renaissance

I am reborn, but never die
I have cleared out all the
Rooms in my mind
Full of trivia, attachments,
Disapproval and pride.

I am twice-born and at peace
Full of joy at the release
Of so much pain.
I open the door marked One
And light from the Universe floods in.

I lived, but scarcely
Now I live completely
Each cell infused with light
Each atom a microcosm of life:
Cascading protons
In a pool of delight
At the deliciousness of life!

Om Shanti (Prayer of Peace)

Body: I've never known ecstasy like this before
To feel no pain or tension
To not feel "in" the body—but something more:
A state of being with no edges or limits
Where Now has no time or place
Where the warmth of belonging is like the
Sweetest embrace
From a parent long-passed
The single tear of joy a longing for grace.

Speech: Let me heal others' wounds with my words
And listen with my heart
Let me remember our threads of connection
And allow others to choose their own paths.
Let me savor the stillness of unimaginable peace
As I reach out to my brothers in times of need.
Lastly (or firstly?) let me say sweet things about me
For self-kindness is the seed
Which provides life to the tree
Of compassion and love.

Mind: Peace. A threefold release
Of body, speech and mind.
When the body is treasured
And our words are measured
Then the mind feels no pressure
To control what will be; content in its purity
This Golden Ticket to Samadhi:
Om Shanti. Shanti. Shanti.

The Lord's Plea

Divest yourself of restlessness
Live life by a higher set of rules
Love me more deeply each day
Forget about your many mistakes
Yet do not forget to give, not just take.
I loved you then, I love you now
And I will love you ever more.
Come back to me Child
I'm knocking at the door.

Treat joys and pain all the same
Remember I am with you
Each step of the way.
I loved you then, I love you now
And I will love you ever more.
Come back to me Child
I'm knocking at the door.

Lay down the saddlebags
Of your woes
Untie the reins of stubbornness
From around your core
Shorten the distance between us
To ease my daily heartbreak.
I loved you then, I love you now
And I will love you ever more.
Come back to me Child
I'm knocking at the door.

Renounce this world
Of pleasure and emotions
Come sit with me in blissful devotion

As we watch time expand
Into nothingness in space:
This tranquil place
Of cosmic synergy and
Softest harmony.
I loved you then, I love you now
And I will love you ever more.
Come back to me Child
I'm knocking at the door.

TODAY: Many people who seek to be closer to God tend to think that they are calling out to Him, praying to Him, asking for His help, but He doesn't answer. What if He *were* calling out to us continually—transmitting like a homing beacon—but that we didn't know how to (or didn't take the time to) listen or make more effort to reach Him. Here are some ways you can do that, although I am sure you can think up your own ways too:

- Start putting into practice what you read in spiritual books (e.g. work on supplanting your ingrained negative habits with new, positive ones; use your skills and attributes to help others).

- Read an extract from a spiritual text every day (this could be the Christian Bible, the Hindu Bhagavad Gita, the Islamic Qur'an and so on) and carry its message with you throughout the day, trying to put it into practice in your daily life.

- Make a commitment to find some time to sit in meditation or prayer. Practice being in the silence and ignoring the chattering mind. Not only does this take you closer to God, it's so good for your emotional, physical and mental health too: in time and with practice, your breathing slows; tension in the muscles dissipates; stress decreases; the mind calms; blood pressure eases. Even a few minutes sitting in stillness can provide clarity to your frazzled, time-pressured mind, and allow for better decision-making.

Hush, Child

You'll have noticed a definite theme running through the poems now of turning inward to find joy rather than (only) perceiving it in the external world through our senses. It's not always easy to find that joy, and in this poem I have cast the egoic mind (that part of us which likes to be in complete control at all times) as an insistent child repeatedly vying for our attention. The ego, with all its wants, needs and opinions, agitates the mind, making it unsettled. We can get caught up thinking about our day, and before we know it, our train of thought has led us on a merry dance, thinking of anything but sitting in stillness trying to meditate! We are taught in meditation to calm the mind so that we can enter a peaceful state within us from which access can be gained to our true Self: the soul. Calming the breath calms the heart. When we are concentrating on breath work (or mantra), this takes our focus away from the external world which we experience through the senses. When we do this, the mind eventually becomes calm. Take it from me, this takes a lot of practice!

Be gentle with the ego for it is part of you yet be firm in your intention to meditate undisturbed by its thoughts of the past or the future or by its incessant wants and needs. If you are interested in meditation, I recommend finding a good meditation teacher or group so that you participate regularly. In this way, you will embed the techniques of breath work, mantras, meditation and prayer. I can say with all honesty that meditation has changed my outlook, my relationships, my emotional health, my physical health—my whole life.

I'm bored. We're not doing anything except sit here. I'm itchy.
Hush, Child.
I'm meditating.

Oh, the film last night was fantastic. That was exciting, wasn't it?

The ending... amazing. I wasn't expecting that. Boom! She was
great, wasn't she? What was her name...?

Hush, Child. None of that matters now.

I'm meditating.

I'm still itchy. Maybe I'll scratch it. And my muscles feel tense.
Perhaps I'll rub them.

Ignore it, let it pass...

None of it matters.

I'm meditating.

Surrender.

Peace envelops me
In a loving embrace;
Love calms me,
Carrying me
To that blissful place;
Light guides me there
In a state of grace.

It does feel nice.

That's it. Hush now.

What are we doing later?

None of that matters.

I'm meditating.

Hush, Child

Yet know that you are loved.

Inner Stillness: the joyful soul dance

(previously published on *Thrive Global!*)

What is inner stillness?

Both feet schlep across the wet floor tiles as I pad my way towards the swimming pool's edge. The familiar smell of chlorine rises up to my nostrils—a sharp frisson of anticipation for the joy to come. Calm waters, barely a ripple disturbing their pristine surface, invite me to join them and my skin displays goose bumps in response.

A sudden liquid cold rushes from feet to chest at the first surrender of the body to the water, then automation takes over, as stroke after stroke I carve a blissful path, counting the lengths, maintaining a relaxed, even speed all the while. It's like a homecoming: body and mind engrossed in the task; and my soul sighs with joy. At one with the water, nothing else matters in this time and motion bliss.

This is my time of inner stillness, when I allow my soul to dance with joy.

Mind over matter:

It's been 9 years since I have swum. Yet nowadays, hampered by ill-health and unable to swim with the physical body, I can still reconnect to those feelings; recreate the experience; be in its every moment in my mind's eye. I swear I can even smell the faint scent of chlorine, so immersed am I in the "virtual" act of swimming!

This is not as unusual as you may think. Many sports people use "mental rehearsal" visualization before competing, and scientific research has shown the effective power which visualization has on the brain. They have found that the brain does not distinguish between *actually* doing something and *imagining* doing it. A 2004 scientific study in Cleveland reported on the increase in muscle power (by as much as 35%) gained after 12 weeks of mentally visualizing muscle contractions!

Inner Stillness—the soul connection:
For many people, their time of inner stillness is also when they connect with the Creator. I'm reminded of a lovely quote from Saint Teresa of Avila:

> *You need not go to heaven to see God; nor need you speak loud, as if God were far away; nor need you cry for wings like a dove to fly to Him; Only be in silence, and you will come upon God within yourself.*
> *Saint Teresa of Avila*

Personally, I find my inner stillness by reliving this happy memory of being in the swimming pool. This is an example of mindfulness meditation, a time when we allow ourselves to be in the present moment. You don't have to be a spiritual person to do mindfulness meditation; you don't have to want to connect with God. Even if you practice this simple (or similar) meditation exercise solely to reduce stress during a busy, rushed day, then your body-mind will thank you.

The power of mindfulness meditation:
Research has shown that regular mindfulness meditation changes the way the mind reacts to previous and future stressors. I'm referencing here an article in *Psychology Today* (May 2013):
"This Is Your Brain on Meditation" by Dr. Rebecca Gladding gives as an example of her findings: "your ability to ignore sensations of anxiety is enhanced as you begin to break that connection between the unhelpful parts of the Me Center of the brain and the bodily sensation/fear centers." The findings go on to say (paraphrased) that regular meditation also helps to form stronger connections between other parts of the brain, meaning that

when you experience bodily sensations—such as pain—you can view them more rationally, from a less anxious, more detached viewpoint, and just let them drift away. This is a very interesting article which I urge you to read as I have heavily redacted it! Suffice to say, mindfulness is not some mumbo-jumbo, new-age, alternative hippy-culture thing (does anyone still think like that?). It is a scientifically-proven technique which is so important to our overall well-being (mental, physical, emotional and spiritual)!

Over to you:
The key is to do your joyful soul dance often; imprint it as a new, positive habit in your mind. Remember you can choose any calming, repetitive activity—painting, running, walking your favorite forest trail, making pancakes and so on—that you can easily recreate in your mind's eye, using the senses to recall all the details. This will help to bring you to a state of inner peace.

Glide

I wrote this poem to sum up how good it feels to be in the moment of inner stillness:

> Kicking off against the side
> I glide; arms outstretched
> No need to breathe
> Just glide, in liquid silk
> Sweet harmony of body and mind.
>
> Where do I end and it begin,
> This miracle skin?
> This mingling of atoms:
> A reaching within.
>
> Ripples become waves
> Then dissipate again.
> I am present in the water
> Yet I leave no lasting stain.
>
> And so I glide, unhurried,
> Through life, as in the water.
> Untroubled by waves
> I simply watch them subside
> And I glide...

♫ *Listen to the audio poem.*

A Mother's Love

As you nestle into my lap
Curled up soft and warm,
Cleansed is my barren heart
Enshrouded no longer
By fear and sorrow.

Tiny, yet with a tsunami's might
Bathed are my soul-wounds
By your tidal wave of love.
Soothed is my restless heart
By the rhythm of your breath.

Tears of joy now
For memories past
Weeping no more now
For things left undone.
Thank you for choosing me,
Little one.

TODAY: Take a minute to pause and think about what it is in your life that melts your heart, or are you still "enshrouded by fear and sorrow", afraid to let others in? Remember, life is a constant cycle of change, and it's how we react to these changes and challenges that determines our spiritual progress, but most of all, it's LOVE that is the driver of everything. There are many types of love (parental, filial, conjugal, friendship, charity work and so on).

Soul Sisters

(This is dedicated to my Friday Meditation Group)

Here we gather
Five as one
Sounding the call
Of the Universe.
Soul Sisters
Encircling with light
Five crystalline shafts
Tethered to the ground
And reaching for the stars.

Chakras aligned
And inner peace found
We hold and behold
The world in our midst
Beaming compassion to all.
This matrix of love
So tenderly woven
This ease of connection.
This bliss.

Soul Sisters,
Raising the vibration
As we sing our way home.

War and Peace 1

War: a bloody impasse between
Sense and nonsense
Normal rules no longer apply
As planes fly overhead
Men lie wounded and dead.

Would that another way were possible
Of peaceful compromise, of entente-cordiale
Between people who are not so different after all.

Our boys deserve to become men
Not casualty numbers soon forgotten
In the everyday chaos of battle.
Let them create future memories now
In the safety and peace of tolerance and love.

Peace: New life springs forth from the tears
Of the Earth
For gentleness and patience heal all wounds.

Resilient shoots emerge after the ravages of fire
In this benevolent field of hope.
Love soothes all anger. Love eases all pain.

Hatred and fear will not take root here
For joy has created this beautiful tapestry
A binding of peoples in peaceful accord
And understanding will its nourishment be.

War and Peace 2

I came across this wonderful quote from Confucius:

If there is righteousness in the heart,
There will be beauty in the character;
If there is beauty in the character,
There will be harmony in the home;
If there is harmony in the home,
There will be order in the nation;
If there is order in the nation,
There will be peace in the world.

Isn't that lovely! However, all across the globe we can see evidence of a lack of *peace*. World leaders fight for the upper hand politically and economically. It was ever so. One of the reasons for this is that many nations lack *order* (unemployment, strikes, tax evasion, inequality of pay/rights and so on). Additionally, for there to be order in a nation, we surely need a certain level of *harmony* in each home of the nation, for is not the home a microcosm of society at large, with different generational stresses and needs? This domestic harmony will be lacking if the people in the home lack *beauty* of character (gentleness, kindness, compassion etc.) and are unable to compromise and show understanding of each other. Where does this lack of spiritual qualities originate? In the heart.

TODAY: Remind yourself that each of us has a level of individual responsibility for societal and global ills. Peace, goodwill, tolerance, understanding, kindness, harmony, compassion all begin at home.

Airs and Graces

Better to forgo our airs and graces
Those follies built on fear
That no-one will love us as we are.

A friend won't mind wrinkles or wobbles of fat
Or the funny way we laugh.

Comparisons with others
And finding ourselves wanting
Is a malady with no cure.

No-one is better or lesser than we
If we learn to love ourselves, then we will see
That the Airs are the Angels' songs
And the Graces God's gifts to us all.

Unimatrix Zero

Fans of the television series *Star Trek* may recognize the imagery of the Borg, a species of man/machine connected to one single neural network (the hive). They need to regenerate every evening, and some find their way to *Unimatrix Zero*, a dream world where they can be free from the shackles of their physical form. I've often thought that the writers of *Star Trek* had Divine inspiration, as their world of magical realism so often echoes that of our world. We are not so different from the Borg!

Unimatrix Zero:
The stuff of which dreams are made.
Disconnected from the hive
To roam free in this other place.

Unshackled by the limitations
Of man-made expectations
We soar and mingle
Finally alive.

Absolute perfection
Of thought and form
Reunited with Source
Our bodies rejoice.

We surrender to this space
Like the softest, sweetest
Lightning bolt of grace.

Our essence is recharged
Our cells regenerated
Our light rekindled
Ready for another day
Of service to the Whole.

The Bothy: a short story

PART THREE: The Dream

Soaring, spiraling higher and higher still, wings precisely balanced, feathered tips reacting instinctively to each whisper of the wind: a masterclass in aeronautical engineering. A bewildered thought brushed his consciousness, "Where was this place?"

Jim felt a tingling sensation on his skin, a fresh, frosty kind of infusion almost—as if he'd walked into a deep freezer. He knew he was on the wing, but they were soundless as they teased the air. A blanket of white encompassed everything in his vision, so that all life appeared to merge as nothingness. He was surrounded by white. No, he was immersed in white. None of this made any sense to him but it felt right to experience what he could only label as emptiness; to align his troubled being with what felt to him like a greater existence or consciousness.

The buzzard—whose body Jim appeared to be possessing temporarily in this most vibrant of dreams—emitted a series of piercing calls which began to soften the ache in Jim's restless heart. With each vibration through the ether he felt something pop, release.

"What is this emotion I am now experiencing?" Jim wondered. "A sense of freedom. Was that it?" His brow creased a little with confusion.

His endless search for happiness out with himself had so far proved fruitless. So many years ingesting the latest ideas on enlightenment, contentment and so on, only for the books to then take their place on the groaning shelves of the bookcase in Jim's study. Yet now, here he was, master of his own dream. He was a magnificent buzzard; the entire sky his domain for the taking. He was free to dance across the blue; free to find the space between duty and living a lie. That last line was just for him.

Duty and living a lie. That was it! He had to empty himself

to find his true Self. His little self was the one playing the parts of Jim the father, husband, colleague, friend, keeping up appearances, working to pay for more things, more experiences. He was tired of it all! What of his true Self? The one who felt the raw ache within, that hole too big to ever be filled. The one who longed for a simpler life; to run outside and inhale great lungfuls of the air after rain; to talk about important things, not holidays and the latest car again.

His feathers suddenly felt heavy with the burdens of the dross he knew had to be disposed of. And so, he released them like stones, to fall as hail and be subsumed into the timeless expanse of white: regrets, anger, moments of spite; judgement, greed and hate.

"Aagh!" He felt the pain shoot down his legs and the breath knocked out of him as he landed on his back out of the rope swing. A distant memory resurfaced of walking into the neighboring town with his father one sunny day. He must have been around 8 years old, and he'd stopped to play on the rope swing dangling mischievously from the lower branch of a sturdy tree. He couldn't resist and, after settling himself on the wooden seat, he began to swing higher and higher.

"Look at me, Dad. I'm soaring like a bird," he'd giggled. His carefree little legs powered his ascent and he leaned back to look at the clouds above. Then *whack!*, the rope snapped and his little body dropped like a stone to the hard root-broken earth below. The memory was so vivid now in every detail, Jim thought, and he remembered that after this point he'd become more averse to taking risks; he'd rushed into growing up; his free spirit had been hidden away in a need to be sensible, for this is how he would avoid hurting himself again, wasn't it?

A gentle hand leaned in to help him. "You alright, man. You let out a terrible scream. Woke me up," smiled Adam.

Jim ran a hand through his ruffled hair and checked his back for any signs of damage from his fall.

"Sorry about that, Adam. I had a very strange dream." He watched a bleary-eyed Adam put another log on the fire and hold up the tea pot.

"I'll make us a cuppa shall I?" (To be continued.)

When the Dust Has Settled

Do not give in to pain today
It passes: like a trail
Of buffalo on the plain
Thunderous and overwhelming
Seemingly endless.

But look behind you now.
There's only dust:
A silent echo of the hurt
That was. Consigned to the past
And soon forgotten.

Discourse on Forgiveness

For – give – ness. I've just realized
it's all about giving.
What shall I give?
Yourself.
To whom shall I give?
To all that Is.
Why is it so difficult to forgive?
Because the ego is wounded.
It seeks retribution.
What if I don't forgive?
A lack of forgiveness causes seeds of resentment
to grow in the heart, hard and impenetrable
like stones. And too many stones weigh us down
slowing our progress on the spiritual path.
How shall I forgive?
With an open heart, with sincerity and
no trace of judgement.
How many times shall I forgive?
A countless number of times.
How may I forgive myself and others freely?
The Universe provides opportunities
for growth. Grab them; analyze your thoughts,
words and actions. Learn from mistakes
and you will improve. But don't give up because
it's difficult!
I'm ashamed of these stones in my heart!
These stones will be flushed out
in the wash of compassion.
Thank you, Guru. I love You.
I love you too, Child.

If you can't forgive, and if your heart is full of hatred for another person or persons who have wronged you at some point in the past, then you are living in darkness, not light—and this never ever brings happiness. In effect, the ego is in control of you and the more you think venomous thoughts about this person, the more the hatred will grow, poisoning your body-mind. This can then seriously affect any of the other systems in your body—circulatory, respiratory, digestive, nervous, muscular and so on. If you are constantly putting out thoughts of hate for others, you amplify them and make them stronger. You also, according to the spiritual law of attraction, bring thoughts of hate your way from others. Therefore, your life will be heading down the road to misery.

We often can't forgive because of how others would view it. We don't want to be seen to be weak or a failure, and forgiving may look as if we have had to concede "victory" to another person. We convince ourselves that we are in the right and the other person is therefore in the wrong. We see things in black and white, instead of the many shades of grey. It also takes two to begin and perpetuate a fight, and if you decide you are no longer going to "fight", where does that leave the other person? They have nowhere to go. If they keep trying to throw hatred and aggression your way and you refuse to retaliate, they will eventually look silly, and hopefully stop!

TODAY: Think about a grudge you have borne for some time. In the grand scheme of things, with all the evil occurring in the world today, does this person or misdeed warrant your continued hatred? Does it matter now? Are you concerned about what others will think of you if you forgive this person? If you decide to release this hatred, and I hope you do, it will bring you immeasurable release. A really effective way to do this is to visualize "cutting the cord" of this hatred as if it were a lead balloon that you have been dragging along behind you in life. Just cut the cord with a pair of imagined shears; you don't need or want that holding you back any longer. Now walk away, feeling much lighter, and forget about it!

Divine Teacher

I was a teacher for many years
Reciting verbs and tenses to ambivalent ears.
But of You, Divine Teacher, I never tire
Reciting Your glories, repeating Your stories.

I see Your wonder in the morning sunrise
Crisp and clear as a starling's call.
I see Your grace in community enterprise
A rewarding of effort for all.

I see Your teaching in kind deeds each day:
The coins in the begging bowl
The clothes to the charity shop
The smile to the waitress
The turning off of the tap.

I aspire to be like You
I admire the very heart of You
I listen for Your guidance in every way
I am Your willing student, Lord, day by day.

Kindness

(first published in *Acts of Kindness from Your Armchair*, Ayni Books, 2017)

When you love without, you thrive within
When you care for others
Your Soul is swaddled
In the arms of the Creator.

Each ripple of your compassion
Fills the Infinite Ocean
Each step you take
To connect with your neighbor
Lightens and brightens your inner demeanor.

No longer will you walk on by, but notice and act
No longer will you make others cry,
But embrace them instead with the
Endless reach of your love.

At each moment,
Recall our Interconnectedness
Remember that We are One.

In this moment,
Know that you are amazing
A blessing from above.

In every moment,
May you choose kindness and love.

Cosmic Vibration

This poem is inspired by the Gayatri Mantra, one of the oldest
(at least 3,000 years) and most powerful of Sanskrit Mantras. It is
a prayer to Brahman (the Supreme Creator) to inspire and guide
our intellect and open our hearts.

Cosmic vibration
Soothing energy from
Benevolent Source
Smoothing the embers
Of chaos and change.

Setting the mind's eye aglow
Causing sparks of cognition
And waves of creation
As this son-et-lumière
Thrums to and fro.

Divine Universal static
Attracting the debris
Of energetic thought.

Take a moment and listen.
Hear with your heart
The machinations of Source
As it sends out its Eternal Om.

Om
Bhur Bhuva Swaha
Tat Savitur Varenyam
Bhargo Devasya Deemahi
Deeyo Yo Naha Prachodayaat.

Live in the Light

I love the imagery in this poem of the mythical Gorgon Medusa, a woman transformed into a Gorgon, complete with snakes for hair and who can turn anyone to stone who meets her gaze. But there is a message here to look behind the fearful monster and try to see the pain. I believe that understanding what makes us fearful is a big step towards forgiving ourselves or others, letting go and then moving on with our life.

Darting amongst the shadows
In our mind
Part of us
Yet abhorred in disgust
The Gorgon of fear
Spreads her rhizome-like tendrils
Around any heart:
A fear-seeking missile
Set to explode on impact.

We daren't look
At this Medusa within
We keep her locked away
At bay, so we think.

Yet, the sweetness of her tone
May turn a heart to stone.
For fear is irresistible
To the ignorant and susceptible
Whose fate is now surely done.

But we can rise above her.
Let love fill our hearts
Feel the tendrils dissolve

Reach out with compassion
To absolve
The Gorgon child
To reassure her
And release her
Into the night.
For henceforth
Shall we live in the light!

Sacrifice

Thank You Lord
For the plants and trees
Which proffer their seeds
That others may feed.

Thank You for the rain
Which falls in Your name
That life may flourish again.

Thank You for the Sun
Which shines its light selflessly
That we may thrive.

Let nature teach and guide us
To use our gifts in service to all.

What use are these talents
If hidden away
That none may see?

What use are these skills
If left to shrivel at will
That none may benefit?

There is great joy in sacrifice
For the benefit of all.
Let us give our time, our patience,
Our money—give it all!

For these things are merely loaned to us
For the greater good of all.

I am trying to be a better person in this second part of my life. I like reading the Gospels from the New Testament Bible and I also love The Bhagavad Gita, a sacred scripture in the Hindu tradition. In both, the spiritual qualities of sacrifice and selfless service to others are emphasized. Christ wanted us to give up everything and follow him. Krishna said there were many ways to follow him. I don't think I'm made for living in a cave and accepting food from strangers, although I have the utmost respect for those who choose that route. In the West, we have to reconcile a need to be secure financially to support our families with the desire to become better, more spiritually developed human beings.

I grew up with the Bible in a Christian family. I came across The Bhagavad Gita 50 years later when my meditation teacher quoted from it from time to time and I was intrigued and interested to read more. I loved it because it felt like the right time for me to ingest its wisdom! In it, we are taught to love everyone as we do our family—unconditionally. If other people misbehave towards us, we should treat them like naughty younger siblings who know no better and show them by example how to behave. If people throw hatred at us, we should return it with love (this is a huge task, and one we all need to work on). This teaching echoes what Christ taught centuries later (Krishna incarnated on Earth in 3227 BCE).

We are also taught to make all our actions sacred, i.e. hand them over as an offering to God. This is what sacrifice is: making sacred. When we do this, what we are really doing is acknowledging that everything we do we can *only do* because of God. He works through us, through our hands, our feet, our minds and so on (He did make us after all!). And if we take it one step further, we realize that as we are all sparks of God, none of us is actually doing anything. It is all God.

TODAY: If you can accept that it is God who is acting through you in everything you do, it will free you, so don't take yourself so seriously. However, that doesn't mean you do nothing! You must still do your duty, for just as the Creator is tirelessly working for our good, he expects you to do the same by using your skills and talents to help others, and not solely those you like. Are you using your skills to help others or just to earn money for yourself and your family? Analyze yourself today on how you measure up to these two spiritual qualities of sacrifice and selfless service and make a mental plan for improvement.

Fibromyalgia... it's a pain! 10 things I do better now.

I wanted to include this Article about Fibromyalgia and how I have come to view it as a gift, a changing of the guard to a different stage in life.

September is Fibromyalgia Awareness raising month in the UK. I want to share with you the 10 things I do better now that I have fibro! If you don't know what fibromyalgia is, it's an illness categorized by constant pain in muscles, joints, nerves as well as overwhelming fatigue at the slightest activity. I have had fibromyalgia and chronic fatigue syndrome (M.E.) for around 9 years. I've run the gamut of emotions in that time, but now I make it my intention to focus on the positive every day (and some days that can be so difficult, but we know, don't we, that we need to ride the storm of bad days in the knowledge that the following day will be better for sure!). In this spirit of positivity, here's a chart tabling what I can no longer do and what I do in its place. I'd be interested in your feedback! I hope it's helpful.

What I can no longer do:	Here's what I do instead:
1. Swim	I take a few moments to visualize swimming and immersing myself in the peace that it can still bring me in my imagination. I wrote a lovely post about just this: Inner Stillness: the joyful soul dance, https://anitaneilson.com/2017/05/22/inner-stillness-the-joyful-soul-dance/.
2. Go for long walks	Go for short walks! We go to our local park in the evening and walk along the tree-shaded riverbank for a few minutes. It's so relaxing. We stop and chat to other dog walkers; we take in gulps of the freshest of air; we peer through the trees to catch sight of the deer. We delight in nature for the short time that we are out in it. Start small and build up a little more each time. I sit out in the garden for a few minutes each day too to bathe my bones with rays of healing sunshine.

What I can no longer do:	Here's what I do instead:
3. Hold down a full-time job	Request a job-share or go part-time, although firstly take a good hard look at your finances to see if you can afford to cut your working hours. If you can, be so grateful that you can and make the right choice for your health. There are plenty of opportunities for volunteering to help others, and I have found that when we are engrossed in helping others, we forget about our pain for a while.
4. Heavy housework	I was unable to do any housework at the beginning of my illness (not so much of a hardship!). Now I can do light housework such as 10 mins of dusting or tidying up. My husband does the heavy work like vacuuming and emptying bins. If you live alone, ask for help from your neighbors or friends. Employ a cleaner once a week if you can. This is also good company for you, especially if you are mostly housebound like me. If you really miss housework (!), you could always spend a few quiet moments visualizing how wonderful it was. Lol!
5. Concentrate in the afternoons	I do any writing in the mornings because I know this is the time I am most alert. For others, it may be the afternoons. Do any paperwork or anything when you need to concentrate (such as make telephone calls) at the optimum time for you and REST at your worst times.
6. Go shopping	I really don't miss shopping. The shopping mall, that cathedral to commercialism. It all seems so unpleasant now. I buy clothes online, making sure I check the size guides before purchasing. If you need to make a return, in the UK it's so easy now to have packages uplifted from home or from local stores.
7. Holidays/ Travelling	I can't do airports (too much stress, light, noise, people, extremes of temperature; just too much of everything, sensory overload); I can't travel in the car more than an hour at a time and when I arrive at our destination, I'm exhausted and need to sleep! So, we tend to go away for day trips to the beach, to seaside towns or to a Farmer's Market, and I always write nice reviews for any places we have visited as an act of kindness. You can make future memories in the small things. You remember the weather, the time for you and your partner to talk, the nice food and good service you had for lunch, the photographs you took and so on. I've visited many places in my earlier life; nowadays I enjoy watching television programs about travel to beautiful places. The brain doesn't distinguish between imagining doing something and actually doing it, did you know that? I find this fascinating.

What I can no longer do:	Here's what I do instead:
8. Knitting	I used to love knitting, but it belongs to the past and to the perfectionist personality that I was (and which still lurks waiting in the background!). There was a lot of ego involved in knitting, that sense of "Oh look what I've created. Aren't I clever!" I was looking for praise from other people and that was all tied up in my lack of self-esteem. Now I know I no longer need others' approval. I can appreciate my niece's knitting achievements, for example ToryaWintersDesigns, but don't feel the need to take up the needles again.
9. Socializing	I can no longer drink alcohol, but you know, I don't miss it. I realized that I relied on alcohol to relax me and I thought I couldn't have a "good night out" without it. Not a bit of it! I can now go out for a short meal in the evening, although I find it very tiring and need to sleep a lot the following day. But it's wonderful to feel connected again with family and friends. If you can't get out, why not invite people to your home, which is what we've done for the past 8 years. By doing this, I could sit and relax on a comfortable chair at home while everyone else organized the meal around me! People are so happy to come and spend time with you, they don't mind if you ask them to heat up some food or make tea. If you've explained your condition, they're happy to help.
10. Driving	I used to love to drive. The freedom that it gives you. I rely on other people to drive me now, although we have recently bought an automatic car which I can drive for a few minutes at a time, but it does cause pain in my arms and I daren't go out at all in the afternoons when concentration is poor. I just wouldn't put others at risk. The thing about driving is, it encapsulates the big thing about having a chronic illness: having to rely on other people. My goodness, how I fought this for years, so determined was I to stand on my own two feet. But it's such a relief when you finally say, "Yes, would you help me with this…" You can still do many things for yourself, but everyone needs a little help with something in their lives. Your pride stands in the way; let it go and you will be happier.

The Waiting

The air has a crispness to it now
As September takes her final bow.
Dawn spreads her misty fingers
'cross the fields and lingers
As I rise to greet the sunrise.

Wrapped in coat and gloves
I venture out to watch the rut
Of the deer, already preparing
For next year.

Life is closing inward
Poised for the waiting of Winter.
There's tidying and sorting,
Preparing and storing
Getting ready for the lean times ahead.

A different phase
In Nature's calendar
Has begun,
With shorter days
And little sun.

Brief moments of activity
Melt in a carpet of tranquility
As squirrels make camp
Ensconced against the damp.

I love Autumn mornings
Full of promise in waiting!

Winter

Introduction to Winter:

When the very breath of Mother Earth herself seems to saturate all living things, crystalizing on plants and trees as if beckoning the next Ice Age. When her spirit permeates the sky, the earth and all spaces in between, accentuating the "absence" of visible abundance and growth experienced in summer. When it is the time to go within, both for the natural world and for ourselves. This is winter: a natural pause for reflection and recuperation before the next wave of growth in spring. This is the duality of life in action. Everything on Earth has its opposite (light and dark, life and death, asleep and awake; and so on) and to experience one aspect we must also experience its opposite. For example, how can we know what being "awake" is really like if we have never experienced what it is to be "asleep"? How can we really experience what "light" is if we have never experienced "dark"? The natural world in winter is a perfect reflection of this great metaphysical pause. Who among us has not stopped for a moment caught in a freeze-frame of scenes, entranced and open-mouthed at the total absoluteness of silence before the onset of a snowfall: the sky leaden with grey, a complete opposite of the vibrant spectrum of colors in summer. When we experience winter, *then* we can really experience and appreciate summer.

Winter's pared-back beauty can be a bleak time for some. For those who have suffered bouts of depression, melancholy and/or Seasonal Affective Disorder (S.A.D.), the dwindling light, the apparent absence of all life, can cause a debilitated mind to spiral even further down into a serious depression, coming to rest in a very dark place where there is no longer even inner turmoil but instead a sense of nothingness: an absence of any feeling, emotion, hope, love, regard, joy. I have fallen down this well many times in the past, and when we do so, we have little desire to pull ourselves back up to the surface, so entrenched are we in the state of nothingness. But pull myself back up I did, many times! One small, tentative step at a time. To survive these bleak times as we perceive them, it's helpful to realize that winter hides her spirit of growth and renewal behind her icy veneer, and we do likewise, don't we, hiding our true colors, beauty and strengths behind the veneer we wish to present to the world! Winter knows that this time of rest and recuperation is a vital precursor to the vibrant, tentative new growth shoots of spring. We ought to follow her example and learn to accept and indeed flourish in the pause.

In the Northern Hemisphere, and certainly in Scotland, where we are much closer to the Arctic Circle than we are to the Equator, we bring artificial forms of light and heat into our homes in an effort to counterbalance the reduction of these in the hibernal natural world: log fires, candlelight, warming, heating drinks with cinnamon and spices to promote heat in the body. We stay indoors out of the cold (our winters are not severe but nevertheless cold, with average temperatures between (-5 to 5C) / (23F–41F). In the UK, hedgehogs, dormice and bats are the only three mammals that hibernate over winter. Hibernation is not sleep; it's a state of decreased metabolism, lowered body temperature, breath and heartbeat. The hedgehog for instance will slow its heartbeat from 190 beats per minute to just 20. Its breathing slows to one breath every few minutes. In this way, it can conserve a huge amount of energy. It survives the lean times of winter on the energy stored as fat in its body.

Similarly, what does the seed do in Autumn to prepare for winter? It begins to withdraw its energy from the peripheries which are no longer required (stalk, flowers etc.) and concentrates its energy and life-force into the core/root. This intense pocket of life-force is not dead, but in a decreased state of metabolism if you like—just like the hedgehog. And this analogy continues with man. In deepening meditation, we learn how to withdraw life-force from the extremities and senses which are not required during the journey within. It's a technique called "pratyahara". The life-force is instead concentrated in the root or core of our being (the soul). As we withdraw the life-force in this way, our breath becomes very slow and easy, our heart rate reduces and we progress from the alpha brain waves of relaxation to the theta waves of deep meditation. This is not sleep but deep, active concentration. We are connected to God (the Creator, Source, whatever name you give it). We are in a state of voluntary stasis where we concentrate our energy at the core of our being, conscious of, but not attached to, our surroundings, using our energy only for the bare necessities of the respiratory and circulatory systems (just like in hibernation), but at the same time ready for action in the external world should it be required.

Instead of resisting winter's period of rest, recuperation and stasis, I've gradually learned to embrace it, taking advantage of the longer evenings of dark to partake in self-reflection; setting goals; deeper meditations and prayer. I think of ways to help others (these are the times when I come up with ideas for fund-raising for example).

The poems of winter reflect a deepening spiritual awareness of the duality of life, of the true nature of life on earth and our role within it, as well as our intrinsic interconnectedness. Poems such as "Under the Dome" which explores the belief that the earth is God's stage and we are the actors on it; "Star in the Darkness" on how to lift the temporary malaise of loneliness. Poignant prayers of longing to be reunited with the Creator ("Peaceful Repose" and "The Siren's Call"). They also reflect growth in meditative practice. What was in the beginning days of spring an exercise in relaxation, has now transformed into a devotional practice not to be missed and given priority at the start of each day. By going within in meditation, the novice spiritual seeker may be rewarded with flashes of light and other audio-visual phenomena, together with increasing levels of inner joy and peace: rewards and encouragement to keep going, for there will be even greater joys ahead if we are persistent ("Metamorphoses" is a lovely poetic example of seeing with the mind's eye and not the two physical eyes; and "The Colors of my Mind" attempts to describe the amazing beauty perceived in meditation). There is so much growth to be experienced under the surface of winter, behind the mask of who we think we are and entwined through these poems is my desire to convey that inner growth.

Choppy Seas

As I can't walk far, my husband sometimes takes me on a short trip to the coast (we only live around 20 minutes' drive away). Sometimes I'll want to visit one of our favorite "tame" beaches where we used to walk our two dogs when they were younger. I have such beautiful memories from those trips: our black Labrador was an incredibly strong swimmer and would relish jumping over bigger and bigger waves to retrieve a tennis ball thrown in for her; the younger dog preferred to paddle along the shoreline, less confident in the deep water. Then it would be time to go home, with the car smelling of damp dogs, snoring contentedly in the back. Simple joy that puts a smile on my face even now. I can still smell the salt air, and the damp dog in car smell; I can still see the sun glistening like diamonds on the sea; I can still hear the occasional airplane taking off from the nearby airport and heading out over the sea to America; I can taste the salt on my lips; I can feel the sand ingressing through my boots and socks to linger in the spaces between my toes. Wonderful!

At other times nowadays, our trips take us to one of the "wild" beaches, and these are to be found mostly further up the coast—my childhood stomping ground. No pristine sand and promenade here, but rather natural harbors and rocky beaches which allow the most amazing displays of wild seas. This is where we parked up one day, watching the hypnotic might of the waves crashing over rocks, powering onshore then dragging themselves back out again, seemingly taking half the shoreline along with them. I am entranced by the sea when it is in such a fiery mood. It makes me feel alive. It also has a certain melancholy to it. Here's the poem I wrote on one such day.

> The seas are choppy today
> A writhing mass of souls forlorn,
> Hissing and thrashing

Their way to the shore.

Lovers lost, fathers gone
Children ever mourned,
Their inner turmoil reflected
In the gathering storm.

This watery vault
Of loved ones' cries,
Is pushed and pulled
By the impatient moon
Climbing its way upwards in the sky.

Gulls shriek in reply
As they rise and fall
Above the angry swell.

The lull comes soon but fleetingly,
And all is calm.
In the stillness the words flow:
"I Am in Everything
Everything is in Me."
"I Am."

Under the Dome

The view from my window is an
Ever-changing palette of hues:

Low, grey clouds drift by on the horizon
Clinging like limpets lest they fall
Tracing the outline of the dome
Under which we thrive.

Beech trees play their concerto of green
In a verdant hello to the skies.
Leaf tips reach upwards
In a natural spire
To join with their neighbors
In this opus of fire.

The blues are the buzzards' domain.
I soar with them in my imagination
Leaving trails of joy in our wake.
As we take to the wing
We hear our souls sing
Releasing the free spirit within.

A dusting of golden sunlight
Finds its mark on the grass
Warming the earth
For the coming of Spring.

What an artist is He
To paint such a canvas
Of beauty upon movement!
What a magical scene,
And it seems so real!

TODAY: The "view from your window" can be influenced by your emotions and feelings at the time. This can present a tainted view of the world, and if you allow this negative opinion to embed itself in your mind, it can become a new belief system, a habit, and one which may be very difficult to supplant. Don't allow entry to negativity! Slam the door in its face. Nip negative emotions and feelings in the bud before they take root.

Blessings

(first appeared in *Fibromyalgia Magazine*, December 2016)

I shimmer with blessings
A swathe of twinkling glee,
Bedecked with decorations
Like the finest Christmas tree.

Not for me
The tinsel and shiny baubles
But the hand-made
Reminders of memories:
Simple expressions
Of how glorious life can be.

I thank You for my sight
That I may see the sky
And my lover's eyes.

I thank You for compassion
Which spreads through my veins
Like sap on the rise.

I thank You for this body
Which does most of what I ask.

I thank You for my friends
Who accept me as I am.

I thank You for my soul,
The strong core within.
Dazzling flame eternal,
More radiant than any bauble.

♫ *Listen to the audio poem.*

TODAY: Create a mental journal of your true blessings in life and say *why* they are so important and precious to you (you could write them down if you prefer). Now, imagine you were living in the aftermath of global war. What would your mental blessings list look like then? How would it have changed? What does this tell you about yourself? This is such a worthwhile exercise to do from time to time in order to keep a check on your priorities in life and to show you how to make progress in your spiritual journey.

Peaceful Repose

I wrote this poem one day when I had been struggling for a week or so with an agonizing amount of pain—much more than normal. There is usually no reason for this increase, despite my spending many hours and days trying to discover a cause (and therefore in my mind, to prevent it reoccurring). It just is. I can fight it and send negative and despairing thoughts out into the ether, or I can accept it and try to ride out the storm until the agony passes with the coming of a new day... before slowly beginning again.

These days, I would say I am 60/40 in favor of riding out the storm. Yet, there are some days when nothing will help: not painkillers, not heat pads, not cold gels, not sleep, not pacing, not rocking, not meditating, not rubbing, not screaming at God, not pleading for help. Some days, I have just had enough and I want to leave this pain-wracked body, because it's too much for me to cope with alone. And that's the most important point. When I'm in despair, I feel as if I'm alone, that there's no-one or no-thing that can help me. Of course, I know that's not true, but despair is an evil unto itself and can envelop the mind in a miasma of madness. Here's the poem.

> These bones are weary
> Of walking on the Earth
> These hands no longer
> Can do man's work
> The longing for home
> Grows stronger day by day
> While night-time brings release
> From intolerable pain.
>
> Wrap me up in the
> Cloak of Thy love

And carry me
Homeward, Lord
Allow me to nestle
In the cup of Thy hand
And sleep, peaceful rest,
In that other land.

I dream sweet dreams
Of blissful reverie
Pain a forgotten memory
Fatigue an unthinkable thought.

Lord, grant me passage
And set me on my way
To a world of peaceful repose.
I pray this, this day.

TODAY: If you are struggling, remember that you are *not* alone. Reach out to people, anyone! It could be a neighbor, a friend, your partner. Let them know that you need help, that you can't cope with the pain today. Ask them to visit, or to say a prayer; ask them to pick up a prescription medicine for you, or anything that might help. There are also numerous help lines you can access. Find out the relevant one for your condition and keep the number close by for times of crisis. Talking to someone who understands may well make the difference to your mental frame of mind and will certainly distract you from the physical symptoms of the pain. Bless you. Be well.

Childhood Blessings

I woke up today thinking that it would be Thanksgiving soon "across the pond" in the USA where some of my relatives live, and it got me thinking about family and how blessed I feel to have been born into my family. Here are some of the many things I am grateful for from my childhood:

- We were born to parents who loved us
- We had plenty of siblings for company
- We had a safe, secure home which was warm and dry
- We had free education and health care
- We had the countryside as our play park
- We had an abundance of water, food and clothes
- We had an abundance of love.

It was pretty idyllic then and now. Thank you for all my blessings from the past. I will cherish my life now and in the future.

Metamorphoses

One hundred million crystals
Tumble from the skies
In a shimmering curtain of
Hibernal ice
To surface as snowdrops in spring.

Ethereal messengers whose
Chrysalised wings
Transform into damsel flies
Caressing the skies
In the warm summer breeze.

Autumnal leaves
Broadcast their wares
As a golden counterpane
On the forest floor.

Climbing aboard
My magical transport
I soar above the canopy,
Transformed into light
On this frosty winter's night.

When Gladness becomes Sadness

How do we cope
When a loved one dies?
We know it's part of life
We all have our demise.

Yet when gladness
Becomes sadness
A self-harming wound
Is wrenched open
And pent-up emotions
Run scared, chased by the
Slavering demons of fear
Casting their trip-wires
To ensnare us in hate,
Anger, disbelief, sadness:
Grief.

I feel these emotions and
Welcome them in
For raw as they are,
These too shall pass
As love is blown in.

Joy at the memories
Will gladden the heart
Acceptance the salve
To heal any wound
Gently stemming the flow
And knitting the scar.

TODAY: If you are grieving for someone, psychologists say that it's much better for your emotional health not to bottle up your emotions but rather to allow yourself to run the gamut of the stages of grief: disbelief, anger, bargaining, depression and acceptance. Not everyone goes through all these stages, and people can move in and out of the various stages before they come to a level of acceptance. Everyone's journey is individual. Everyone goes through it at some stage in their life. Gather a support network around you of loved ones who are happy to sit in silence or talk things over with you and/or support you in whichever ways *you* need.

And remember also that we can experience these same stages of grief for other losses in life: loss of good health, loss of employment, and so on. These are challenging times of change presented to us in life as opportunities to learn how to deal with them in positive ways. So, welcome the emotions of grief, for "these too shall pass as love is blown in."

"It is in Giving that we Receive,"
St. Francis of Assisi

(previously published on my blog, *Healing Words*, December 2017)

St. Francis of Assisi was born into a wealthy Italian family (around 1181). After an early life of privilege and experience of war, he turned to God. His later life was one of renunciation, poverty, healing the sick and preaching the word of God. His followers became known as "Franciscan friars", an order which still exists today.

The Prayer of St. Francis, from which the title of this post is taken, is one of his most celebrated poems/prayers. I love it. It sums up how to live a good life by helping others rather than focusing on ourselves. It's Winter here in Scotland and Mother Nature's chilly, icy grip has been tightening throughout the month of December. I woke up this morning in my snug, warm bed with warm gas-fueled radiators heating the whole of our home. Was I ever grateful for the gift of heat when I peeked out of the blinds to see the frosty field opposite, the driveway twinkling its icy warning and the early-morning dog walkers' breath rising like comical chimneys skyward.

So grateful was I for all my blessings this morning. I am every morning anyway, but I was especially thankful today for:

- a warm, safe, secure home;
- a strong body and mind to allow me to thrive in this physical world;
- people who love and care about me;
- a growing compassion for others arising out of moments of personal suffering.

Yesterday, I noticed the horses in the field, wearing their winter blankets, happily munching away on the remnants of grass.

Someone had been thinking of their comfort, their basic need to be warm in a cold climate.

It got me thinking of the cold snap of weather and of those people who don't have a warm home or enough warm clothing. So, I rummaged through my wardrobe and looked out some warm clothes (knitwear, hats, scarves, coats and so on) to donate to a local homeless charity, The Salvation Army. It's just a little thing, but it's all the little things added together which bring big changes, isn't it? No act of kindness is ever too small in my book.

This morning I said to God, as is my wont, "How can I help people today?" When we blog, it's one way of helping people, by sharing our thoughts and ideas on how we can make a big difference with lots of small things. If you live in a cold climate and are blessed to have safety, security and warmth but don't have any items of clothing to donate, you could perhaps think about one of the following:

- donate your time (in prayer or meditation, sending out good positive energy to those in need);
- donate your time by helping out for an hour at a local food bank or homeless charity;
- make a financial donation to a local or global cause that resonates with you. Any amount, however small, is gratefully received and always makes a difference.

I'm not writing this post to make you or I feel guilty about our blessings in life. And if you think you don't have any blessings, you're not thinking hard or smart enough! This morning, I felt I was given a little Divine nudge to do something for others, so I thought I'd share this with you. Please like and share this post if you agree. God bless you. Namaste! Anita.

The Book of Life

I turn the page on this book of life
And step gaily onto the line
Next but one.

Although nearing its end
This tome has just begun
To reveal its complexities
And niceties,
Subtleties and fripperies.

I feel each word with
A slight trace of hand
Like braille imprinted
On my memory.

Sweetness and lightness
E'er prevail
The acrid bitterness
Of spite assailed
In chapters past.

Foes unimagined
Have vanished from trace
For these were mere
Musings of emotions
On speed.

The pages slip through my fingers
A timely reminder of how
Fragile life can be.

This book is a sacred scripture

To be treasured forever
And filed with all others
In the Records Hall of Life.

Take control of the senses

One reason why life has been a struggle for me at times is that, like many of us, I have tried to make sense of it all through the senses. These are the primary conduits through which the stimuli of the world can enter our body-mind. We see, hear, feel, taste, smell, touch. This sensation triggers a thought or an emotion. We either like it or dislike it. This in turn helps to form our opinions and habits moving forward. I'm sure this sensory "dependence" if you like lies at the root of many of my bad habits, such as eating way too much sugar, a tendency towards impatience, intolerance, and a need to try to control life.

My habits were formed in great measure from desires: desires for material things, and these eventually caused havoc and disruption to my mental and physical serenity. Perhaps you're saying to yourself, "What is she talking about?" But think about it for a moment. To give you an example. You taste alcohol. This triggers an emotion (like!). So, you drink more alcohol since you found it pleasurable. A desire for more alcohol is triggered, and so on and so on, and your drinking becomes a habit before you are even aware of it. What if your desire for alcohol is thwarted in some way? This triggers a negative emotion (frustration?), and if this negative emotion is permitted to ferment, it can transmogrify into anger and even hatred. In my view, nothing causes the same degree of havoc and disruption to our mental and physical serenity—and that of other people—as does anger!

Here's another example. Imagine all the sensory agitation we experience from a roller-coaster ride or an all-you-can-eat buffet! Yes, it can be really exciting at the time but as soon as it's over, we crash back down to "boring normality". And so, we continue with this roller-coaster of emotional reactions to sensory stimuli, again and again as we navigate through life. After a while, some of us may tire of this exhausting way of living, and we seek another, calmer way. This way is linked to the interiorization I talked about in the Introduction to Winter. I have become calmer, and now walk a more "even" path by learning to control the senses. It has been described as like keeping a very firm rein on five headstrong horses that are pulling the chariot that is your body. Each of the horses is a sense and is trying to pull us this way and that. The senses have been given to us to be used, but to be used with *wisdom*, turning their focus inward. This happens mostly during meditation, when we tune out to the world and tune in to God (Source, Universal Consciousness, Brahman, Divine Goddess, whatever name you give Him/Her). We don't need to be aware of external sensory stimuli when we are meditating. The peace of "disconnecting" for a while is sublime and envelops you like a blanket of peace, joy, silence, love. Who wouldn't want to live in that way? The ultimate aim for many of us is to also be able to live in this calm, unaffected way in the external, material world. That's a work in progress for me!

If you wanted to try this, you could aim to exercise restraint of the senses by taking one per week to focus on. Don't try to tackle them all at once, as long-ingrained (poor) habits are especially difficult to supplant. So, for example, one week you may want to pledge to control the sense of taste. Perhaps you know you have a craving for sweet foods, despite realizing that their pleasure is short-lived and ultimately disruptive to your bodily health. Psychologists have found that repeating positive affirmations many times a day can be extremely beneficial to our attempts to establish new habits. Try the affirmation below or use one of your own, but also take practical steps to help you in your goal, such as stocking up your food cupboards and fridge-freezer with healthy snacks.

Affirmation: I choose to nourish my body-mind with healthy food!

Star in the Darkness

We all feel loneliness from time to time. Many of us can even feel lonely in a room full of people! I have found that shifting the focus from my own worries to other people helps to lift the temporary malaise of loneliness, for in reality we are none of us alone. We are all interconnected. Use the digital world carefully, avoiding any forum of negativity. Instead, seek out like-minded people and forge new links of friendship in positive, loving, supportive ways. We each have unique talents. Use yours in service to others. Think about how you can help them, because in this way you will also help yourself. Your mood and your soul will be lightened!

Loneliness.
The great void within
A darkness with no stars
To light the way through.

This loneliness
Is a physical-ness
A longing to touch
And be touched: proof
That we are alive
That we matter.

But what if this longing
Is a cry for meaning?
A need to belong and
Be part of the One?

This digital age is a
Matrix for friendship
An energetic belonging

In a non-physical way.
We are all interconnected
Part of the whole
So, reach out and touch it
Establish new links.

Fill the void within
And light the way for others
Be a star in *their* darkness
Let them know that *they* matter.
Today.

Make someone smile
With the light from your heart
And make loneliness
A forgotten moment
In a wonderful day!

The Timeless Place Within

Why do we hurry through life
When it is to be savored in the moment?
Why do we race along,
Stubborn and headstrong,
Missing acts of loving kindness
Happening in our midst?

Pressures of time are merely
Poor habits ingrained in the mind.
We don't need to clear every hurdle
So, knock a few over!

If others mind that we can't manage time
Just leave them behind!
The hare may win the race
But the winner's podium can
Be a lonely place.

So, make like the tortoise,
Slow and serene
Enjoying the journey
Immersed in the scene.

Tranquility is a timeless place
Let it envelop you in its grace.

Faith

The words that we share
Are food for the Soul
Nourishing the Spirit
Invoking peace.

The prayers that we share
Are the sweetest nectar
Prized by the hummingbird
Instilling grace.

The faith that we share
Is Infinite in its beauty
Endless in its humility
Quenching our thirst
For a return to Source.

Our faith is primeval
Transcending all boundaries.
Our belief is immortal
Like our Souls:
Swathed in a cocoon of humanity
Till Ascension beckons
In a concerto of bliss.

♫ *Listen to the audio poem.*

A Moment of Connection

Christmas lights and tinsel brightly
Shimmering on this cold winter's eve.
Small children's eyes, glassy with fatigue
Yet too excited to give in to sleep
Tug their parents' hands with impatient glee.

Crepes are flipped by seasoned chefs
To the ravenous whoops of queuing guests
Ready to savor each sensory delight
Of the Christmas market this December night.

Moments of happiness and
Memories to treasure
Succumb to the infusion
Of sensory pleasure.

But look, tucked away
In a corner out of sight
Is a neon-lit stable
With Baby Jesus,
Two donkeys and Angels
And a flickering "Merry Christmas" sign.

An old man stands before it
Entranced by the scene
The expression on his face
So calm and serene.

I stop for a moment
And share in his wonder.
The world in slow motion,
No row or commotion can

Disturb this peace:
A brief moment of
Connection and reflection
Before returning to the feast.

This poem reminds us not to become too attached to the sensory pleasures of the world, for the happiness they bring is fleeting!

TODAY: Notice when you are on the sensory roller-coaster, stop what you are doing and pause in stillness. Be still for even a few seconds and go within. Calm your breathing, close your eyes if you can, and repeat a mantra such as "I am calm. I am a child of God." This will help to center you and disconnect you from the fickle world of sensory illusion.

Mother Gita

Mother Gita O dearest one
What wisdom shall you impart
From the treasured pages
Of your kingdom?
Silken oracle of wonder
Each timeless sentiment
Flows through my veins
Like rain on parched earth.

And dearest Arjuna
Anxious seeker of knowledge
I recognize in you the spirit in me.
Let us march on our journey together
For as One we are stronger.

The battle is not yet won
But our strength is a tender web
Of compassion for all
And our love for Mother Gita
Is our golden chariot.

Starlight

Twinkling little stars
Blinking in and out
Of existence
In our dimension
Like soft angelic kisses
To take the breath away.

Prana suspended in the air
Thrumming with the power
Of the Universe
Like a nuclear backwash
To immerse our cells in light.

Awareness of awakeness
Bliss in His blessings
Gratitude for God's grace.
This is the stardom I seek!

The Siren's Call

I was born into a God-loving Catholic family. We were brought up to believe in God, to be kind; we were taken to church every Sunday and other holy feast days. We followed the traditions of our religion like not eating meat on a Friday and saying our prayers at night before bed. In my twenties, when other responsibilities and leisure activities took up my time, I decided I didn't need God. I was happy as I was! Then—like everyone else—challenges beset me and I became angry with Him. I can look back now and shake my head and smirk a little at the childish ignorance and arrogance of the person I was in my youth. What was it Jesus said about those people who orchestrated his death, "Forgive them, Father, for they know not what they do." But we are like children spiritually when we've turned away from Him. We end up not knowing how to live our lives and getting it all wrong in the process!

I certainly wasn't expecting to come back to God. I believed I was living a "good" life until ill-health struck in my mid-40s (see "My M.E. Story" in the Spring section). I began meditation classes simply to help me relax. I didn't for a minute think it would reignite the Divine spark within me (which I now know *never* goes out). Yet before I knew it, I was also writing poetry, firstly about the joys of the natural world, and then it became deeper, more turned towards God. It became the outward reflection of a growing inner longing in my heart for God. This took me completely by surprise. Was it Him that I'd been looking for all these years after seeking happiness in material wealth and status and finding it wanting? My longing was transmitting more and more strongly, like a relentless beacon in the fog strengthening my link with the Divine.

It feels different this time though: not a return to organized religion and following its traditions by rote, but a new, individual relationship where I take inspiration from the best parts of

Christianity, Buddhism and Hinduism. My prayers have been answered in an increasing peace, contentment and joy. I realize that God was always listening, but I had tuned Him out! The call home is the sweetest song ever, wordless yet saying so much! My heart is bursting with joy and anticipation. I'm like a little child, desperate for the Father's love. My old life just doesn't hold any interest for me now. I am happy as I am.

I hear the call home
That quiet, persistent beacon
Through the fog
At times loud and strong
At others quiet and soft.

Like a Siren, it sings
In tune with my heartbeat
Enticing me home.
But I can't come yet.
For I've found Your bliss on Earth!

May I continue Your work?
For there are others to help.
May I seek out new places?
For there are wounds to heal.
And when Your work is done
I will race to You with open arms
And cry, "I'm home. I'm home!"

▶ *Watch the video poem.*

Credo

(respectfully based on the Nicene Creed)

I believe in one God
Of many names and faiths
Absolute Creator of all that is.

I believe in Ascended Masters
Teachers of His word on Earth.

I believe in the Divine Mother
Selfless servant to all
And in the Holy Spirit
Igniting the spark in our soul.

I believe in You, Father.
My memory has cleared
Familiar truths unlocked
From the sleepwalking
Malaise of past years.

TODAY: Remember that all religion is man's attempt to find his way back to God, and all paths lead there eventually, so please respect others' religions. You may not agree with them in totality, but equally there may be many areas of commonality between your faiths. Try to meet people halfway in a spirit of understanding and tolerance.

Maya

Sweetest delusion of truth
The Creator's fairy tale of dreams
We wander this realm,
Somnambulant,
Entranced by the bliss
Of ignorance.

Yet the sweetest of fruits
Will rot before long
And fairy tales
Can often be grim.

We've forgotten who we are
And, like Peter,
Thrice we deny Him.
Our dream world
Is an unhappy nightmare
Without God at its core.

So, wake up and offer
Yourself to Him freely
Above all the delights
Of this magical world.

TODAY: Not everyone believes in God. They say, "Oh but you can't see Him. How can He be real?" Well, you can't see the wind, but *it's* real. You can't see most cancers, but *they* are real. It all comes down to faith, doesn't it? I have faith that He is there, the overseer of all, patiently waiting for us to realize this great truth. He has given each of us the gift of free will to choose either the temporary delights of the material, physical world, or the deeper, inner delights of communion with Him. I know which one I'm choosing!

High on Happiness

(published on *Inspiremetoday.com*, November 2017)

"So many silly wasted years trying to find happiness in all the wrong places." That's what I tell myself these days. Advice to my younger self (if I were to listen!) would be: "You don't need to smoke, or drink or go out clubbing, or adorn yourself in diamonds and drive around in a new sparkly car, go on expensive holidays you can't afford and think only of yourself all the time." Phew! All that pressure to conform and be like others and have others like you! It was so exhausting!

Unveil the real you.

Why not discard this mask of unhappiness and reveal the real you. This takes courage, but know that the real you *is* loved, lovable, worthy, kind and so much more than the external trappings of youth which eventually fade. Will you be ready for that, because I wasn't! Will you be ready to love the real you inside? Because I wasn't. Do you know what or who that is? Because I didn't!

"Yes, but the excitement of the chase and the purchase was good, wasn't it?" I hear you say. But how long did it last before the "high" faded and discontent crept in, wrapping its restless tendrils around you, squeezing out every last drop of temporary happiness? Stop doing it to yourself. Now's your chance to change. Get high on inner happiness. Below is one of my favorite quotes from Rumi (a 13th C. Persian poet and theologian). Use it as an affirmation to turn your life around. Remember that each one of us on Earth is distinct, and we each have our own journey to follow through countless incarnations, gradually awakening to the realization contained in Rumi's quotation. Much love, Anita.

The universe is not outside of you. Look inside yourself; everything that you want, you already are.
Rumi

The Colors of my Mind

This poem reminds us that our physical eyes and this physical world are not the only way we see. Through meditation, I have discovered amazing beauty with eyes closed. Try being still and quiet for a few moments today and let the mind take you to a beautiful sanctuary of your imagination.

Do not pity me
If my eyes are sealed
Shut to the outside world.
For the realm
Behind these shutters
Is a kaleidoscope of beauty.

I sit on a lotus blossom
In my mind
Cast adrift in ecstasy
In a timeless space
Where joy is pink and green
And every color in between.
Where beauty is an
Endless emoticon.

I am submerged
In this cosmic bliss.
I am this celestial pulse.

Would that you could see
The beauty within me
And feel every color
In my heart!
Prize open the eyes
Of your soul

And discover the beauty
That you own.

First Born

Thank you for choosing us
And permitting us
To learn:
How to care through you
Make our mistakes with you
And open our hearts to you.

Our time, though years,
Seems fleeting.
Your grace and patience
Unending
Your beautiful, kind soul
Mending all scars
Reminding us daily
To be joyful and silly.

We release your soul
To return home
And continue its journey
In spirit.

But we *shall* meet again
And embrace you again
So entwined are we for eternity.

The Divine Highway

Take the scenic route
On the divine highway!
Slow down
See the abundance of creation.
Accept challenges
And seek to grow.
Be patient
For time is merely
A man-made invention.
Be tolerant of others
Changing their direction.

May your journey
Be steady and calm.
May you welcome diversions
As moments of fun.
And who knows what lies
Behind the setting sun?

So, keep going on the highway
Knowing that the journey
Is the key
To unlocking the prize
Of the final destiny:
Heaven on Earth
Not a place—
But a state of being!

Pain

Pain is an illusion
Rise above it
Stand back and observe
How this body/mind
Endures it.

What does it do?
What does it learn?
To whom does it turn for help?

Pain is a worm-hole
Returning to Source
Cascading and careering
Through time and space.

Whizzing through bones
Tearing through veins
Turning the norm inside out
Until, with an agonizing scream
It comes to rest.

TODAY: Pain comes in all forms: physical, mental and spiritual. Remember that every person you meet today is likely to be enduring pain of some sort, and just as they can't see your pain, neither can you see theirs. Treat others with compassion therefore—as you would like to be treated. When you find yourself making assumptions or judgements about people you meet based solely on what you can see with your physical eyes, stop and rewind your thoughts! Try to put yourself in their shoes and see the world from their viewpoint.

The Bothy: a short story

PART FOUR: The Resolution

"So, there I was soaring over the landscape, completely free. It felt amazing." Jim was describing his dream to Adam who was nodding and emitting grunts of agreement from time to time.

"And I finally got it!" he squealed. "I had to empty myself to find my Self."

"Yeah, like the prayer of St. Francis," Adam piped up enthusiastically. "You have to die to the self to be born to eternal life. In other words, you need to realize that this self, this personality, this body, it's not who *you* are. You are an immortal soul. You're just using this body for a while."

"Yes! And I think I found my soul, up there in the blankness," Jim nodded his assent, beaming. "It was as if I had to come all the way out here to find it."

"That's awesome, man. The trick is to keep hold of that feeling when you come back down to Earth and go back to your normal life. That's when life becomes good."

Adam's cheeks were flushed with what almost appeared to be a sense of pride, Jim thought, or could it just be the log fire which was blazing hot now, with honey-colored flames crackling and spitting as they hastened up the chimney breast.

"I'm glad you were here with me, Adam. I'm glad I wasn't on my own, like I thought I wanted to be." Jim looked sheepishly over at his companion and shifted a little on his seat.

"You're welcome, Jim. Where else would I be?"

What an odd thing to say, thought Jim, and he voiced his confusion across the darkness.

"Haven't you realized who I am yet?" asked the younger man.

"Er, no." Jim's hesitant reply vibrated through the air.

"You will." Adam gave a broad smile. He noticed Jim stifling a yawn. "Let's get a few more hours' sleep and see what the morning brings."

"Thanks, Adam. 'Night," said Jim.

Next morning Jim awoke to the cry of the buzzards overhead. Adam must be out getting water from the stream, he thought, noticing that the bothy was missing his companion. He settled himself at the table and smiled with contentment. He could see his way ahead now, in no short part due to Adam. He felt happy.

"What's this?" Jim noticed a book on the bothy floor and bent to pick it up. *Power Animals* was emblazoned across the front. He could still hear the buzzards' calls overhead, so he decided to look up Buzzards. Flicking through the pages he came upon an explanation for buzzards/vultures. It read as follows:

The Buzzard symbolizes the cycle of death and rebirth. It aids in purification of the mind, body, spirit and in illumination of the way ahead. It asks you to use all your skills and past experience to decide on the highest path for you, allowing you to soar above your perceived limitations. The Buzzard comes at times of change and transformation, helping you to awaken to your higher possibilities.

With a wry smile, Jim packed up his things and, easing the door shut behind him, he turned to go home. THE END.

The Delights of this World

Isn't it amazing that every single person on Earth is different (identical twins notwithstanding)! I used to try to be like other people, thinking that this would make others like me. I spent many years comparing myself to others and finding myself wanting. If only I was as wealthy as them; if only I had a lovely car like them; if only I was as clever as them; and so on. I tortured myself with this unkind behavior, because the reality is that no matter how hard you try, you cannot possibly be the same as other people. We are all different, and this fact is something to be celebrated not feared!

I thought I was so tolerant of others' differences until a recent stay in hospital, when this tolerance was sorely tested. A Muslim asylum seeker was brought into the cardiac ward and into the women's ward specifically, since there were no beds available in the men's ward. His son was with him and insisted on staying with his father during the night. He planned to sleep on a mattress on the floor in the ward. They talked in Arabic. This completely freaked me out and revealed an innate bigotry I didn't even know was there. Would I have behaved like this if they were British and white? I don't know. Was it because they were men and I felt uncomfortable? Yes, partly, but really it was because they were Muslim; they were foreign. I didn't know how to act around them. I didn't know what to expect from them. I couldn't communicate with them. I feared them.

I'm quite shocked at my behavior as I look back at it. I was so lacking in compassion for this man who had obviously had a problem with his heart and was feeling vulnerable. Perhaps his culture separated men and women socially. If so, he must have felt extremely uncomfortable being placed in a women's ward. Eventually, he was moved to a side room and another man (who was Scottish) was brought in to the women's ward in his place. My relief was almost palpable.

Now, I am well-read in spiritual matters. I know that this person that we inhabit is not the real "us". We are the immortal soul housed in the body. Therefore, we are male, female, Scottish, Syrian etc. only for this lifetime. We are all God's children. We are all interconnected. But I didn't feel that at the time. I'm glad I was given this challenge to see how I would cope with it. I feel that overcoming bigotry with understanding is a major lesson I need to learn in this lifetime. I need to hand this bigotry over to God. But how can I stop this fear of others and lack of understanding in its tracks? By finding out more about them; by meeting them; by hearing their stories; by realizing the many commonalities we have between us and so on. In any case, here is the poem about diversity. I hope it resonates with you.

I see a world where diversity
Flows from a candy-stripe river
In a mouth-watering mix of
Color and form.

Each gem
Ready to be savored
An exquisite mélange
Of disparate flavors.

I see a world where rainbow clouds
Drip honey-hued rain
On all kinds of terrain,
Offering themselves
In service to all.

I shower this world
With the light from my heart
For it gladdens my soul
To see love in its path.

Love has no borders,
Boundaries or barriers.
Love accepts all creeds,
Customs and colors.

See not with your eyes
But with your heart
And the delights of this world
Will be strewn in your path.

TODAY: Read the last two paragraphs again. Don't allow bigotry to reign within you. Battle it with the power of love! Learn from my mistakes. Be understanding of others and shower them with love.

Christmas wishes

I don't need any more sparkly gifts but it's lovely to receive them all the same. But for me this coming year, it's important to give as well as take. Here are three ways to give more this Christmas:

- consume less (that means less shopping from that large on-line retailer with its mountains of unnecessary packaging!!);
- share more (stop holding on to money, time, things—just give); and
- recycle and upcycle more instead of just throwing things away and buying shiny new replacements.

It's nearly Christmas and I wish you all the most joyful of holiday times with family around you. Remember, next time you tut at whiskers left in the sink, be grateful that you have him; next time you get annoyed at the dogs barking, be grateful that you have them; next time your body lets you down, be grateful that you have it all the same. Much love! Anita.

Homecoming

I will bring Your people
To You Lord
I will bring them to You
With these words
Softly and quietly
Imbued with Your love
Sweet lyrics of Angels
Divine gifts from above
Celestial reminders
Beckoning us home
To merge with the Oneness
That is You.

Doorway to Everlasting Bliss

When we meditate steadfastly, each and every day, ideally twice a day, we are rewarded with gifts from the Creator:

Silence, when the body is relaxed and the mind is quietened;
Peace, when we can maintain a still body and mind;
Joy, when we take the next step closer to God. This is when we connect with our true self: our soul.

Remember, this body-mind, with all its opinions, personality traits, strengths and foibles, is how we have chosen to appear during this lifetime. The real "us" is behind all this window dressing which merely enables us to function in the world of earthly matter. St. Francis called his body "Brother Donkey" for he knew its sole purpose was to transport him around on the earth. We are spiritual beings, immortal. How lovely is that! When we meditate and can reach this state of bliss, we have re-connected with our soul and with the Supreme Creator.

The next step is to transpose this blissful state into our daily lives. This we do by remembering God throughout the day (loving him with our hearts, minds, thoughts, acts), by serving others selflessly and by treating others as we would want to be treated. This is the path to everlasting bliss. Namaste.

Deep Silence:
The other-worldly world of bliss
Glorious sanctum of Heaven.
The boundless place
Where Infinity persists
In wondrous elation.
Whom shall I call in this

Hall of Cosmic reflection?

Deep Peace:
A timely release
Of body and mind.
A chance to greet the soul
In all its perfection and might.
A journey of resilience
Of mind over matter.
Peace: His appreciation
For our demands for attention.

Deep Joy:
Walking through the doorway
To everlasting happiness.
Hearing the sound
Of Cosmic connections
Vibrating, thrumming
The Universal Aum.
Seeing Thy light
Through the eye of wonder.
Feeling Thy presence
In the silence of peace.

I give myself to Thee freely, Lord
How may I serve Thee
Today with my words?

Shall I bring comfort to others
And light up their way?
Shall I love them as brothers
To ease their journey?

For the love in my heart
Is a powerful searchlight
And like moths shall they come
To feast in its delights.

Rebirth and Renewal

I sit here pondering
The meaning of life
As raindrops are showering
The plants outside.

All contraction released
By these powerful waters
As life is reborn
With shoots
'neath the surface.

Life and rebirth:
A continuous sigh
A celestial gift
That we might try
To supersede
These material binds.

Born afresh
With new hearts
New minds.

Yet the soul remains:
Irrefutable link to the Divine
To continue its journey anew
From our end-point last time.

The longing in my soul, Lord
Is to come home to You.
The yearning for salvation
And cosmic repose

In the realms of creation
Grows ever close.

Let me sit at Your side
And forever there abide.

I See You Now (Reprise)

I see You now
That nebulous twilight
In my mind
With glimpses of light
So wondrously bright
In this most tenuous of realms.

I hear You now
That eloquent voice
In my head
Crisp and matter-of-fact
As worldly chatter ebbs.

I smell You now
In the scent of rose
Pervading my senses
As spirit draws close.

I feel You now
In observing this life
From a state of
Gentle wonder and delight.

I taste You now in
Life-giving prana
Of thought-made-light.

I touch You now
In the folds of Your robe
As I sit in peaceful satsang
In Your presence once more.
I see You now.

I see You now.
I see You now.

About the Author

Anita Neilson is an author, spiritual poet and blogger. A graduate in 3 modern languages, she travelled, lived and worked in Europe before careers in business and education in Scotland. She is now a self-employed writer, contributing to many mind, body, spirit and chronic illness publications.

Anita lives in the lush, verdant countryside of Ayrshire, in the west of Scotland, where the beauty and diversity of the natural world provide inspiration for much of her writing. Kindness, compassion and leading a positive, spiritual life are upmost to her. Anita has Fibromyalgia and M.E. (Chronic Fatigue Syndrome) and her husband is her caregiver and inspiration for many an act of kindness.

Other books by the Author: *Acts of Kindness from Your Armchair* (Ayni Books, 2017).

Contributing Author to *Goddess: When She Rules* (Golden Dragonfly Press, 2017).

Her blog and poetry aim to teach others:
- how illness can be a blessing, presenting us as it does with opportunities for soul growth (such as increased compassion for others' suffering);
- how we can distract the mind from pain and fatigue through the healing power of positive thoughts and words; and
- how we can all make a meaningful contribution to the world simply by reconnecting with our inner compassion and love.

Connect with Anita:
Healing Words blog http://anitaneilson.com
http://www.facebook.com/AnitaNeilsonAuthor
http://www.instagram.com/soulmurmurs

Other Books by the Author

Acts of Kindness from Your Armchair
Ayni Books 2017. ISBN: 978-1-78535-617-9

An exploration of how we can make a meaningful contribution to the world through simple acts of kindness, all easily done from home. The book acts as a practical guide to the ways in which thoughts, words and acts of kindness, both inward and towards the wider world, can create real change. It leads us on a journey from compassionate self-analysis and meditation; kindness towards others both in person and online; kindness towards the animal kingdom and finally caring for the planet—one little step after another! This toolkit of ideas and practices arose from the author's personal experiences in her quest to find a new purpose in life, despite health limitations, through the power of kindness.

"We can all make a difference, regardless of any 'limitations' we may have, whatever our circumstances. In my experience all 'big' things happen through lots of small things, and this book is a great reminder of the big difference that small everyday acts of kindness can make."
Karen Darke MBE, Athlete and Adventurer, Paralympic Champion 2016. Author of *If You Fall* and *Boundless*.

"A spiritual guidebook for harmonious living."
Catherine L. Schweig, Editor of *Bhakti Blossoms, Journey of the Heart* and others.

"Inspires the reader to achieve a happier, more fulfilled living and open up to positivity, peace and natural well-being."
Fotoula Adrimi, Director ISIS School of Holistic Health.

"This is also great for other people who want to help but have no idea where to start."
Dawn's Reviews.

Goddess When She Rules
Golden Dragonfly Press 2017. ISBN: 9780998976655

Contributing Author in this extraordinary collection of poetry and prose penned by spiritual women across the globe in an exploration of what the Goddess energy signifies to them.

Coming Soon

Rose Petals Floating Downstream
A collection of beautiful, spiritual poetry from the heart, exploring all aspects of the Divine: in the natural world, through the senses, in meditation, through our daily lives, and in the inner world of silence, peace and joy.

Note to Reader

Thank you for purchasing *Soul Murmurs*. I hope that your soul feels "enlightened" and that you have gained as much from its reading as I did from its creation. If you have a few moments, please feel free to add your review of the book on your favorite online site for feedback. Much love. *Anita Neilson*

Glossary

Arjuna: The protagonist of The Bhagavad Gita (see below). Arjuna symbolizes all spiritual seekers.

Ascended Masters: Spiritually enlightened beings who have worked out all their past karma, left the cycle of rebirth and reached full union with Universal Consciousness (Ascension). These include Jesus Christ, Lord Krishna and Sri Yogananda.

Audio poems: See *Healing Words* blog Audio page: http://anitaneilson.com/audio/

Aum: The Universal Aum (A = creative energy; U = maintaining energy; M = destructive energy). This is the energy of thought and form created by Source (the Creator, God) which permeates all life. Often written as Om.

Aurora: Goddess of Dawn in Roman mythology. Said to fly across the sky each morning in her chariot, to announce the arrival of the sun, wearing a purple cloak which trails in her wake.

Bhagavad Gita (The): Often affectionately called Mother Gita is a holy scripture predating the Bible. Written in Sanskrit (there are many translations available), it details the spiritual journey of its protagonist, Arjuna, as he battles against those aspects of the self (our negative tendencies) which prevent us from realizing our true nature. Lord Krishna lovingly guides him to greater clarity on his spiritual journey. The chariot symbolizes the physical body, and the battlefield is the mind.

Celtic: Legacy of the Celtic peoples who lived in northern Europe in Roman times. Modern-day Celtic nations/peoples include, in the UK: Scotland, Wales, Isle of Man, Ireland and Cornwall;

also Brittany (France) as well as Galicia and Asturias (Spain) and northern Portugal.

Confucius: Chinese philosopher, born in 551 BCE.

Divine Mother: The feminine aspect of God in the Hindu tradition.

Gawain: One of King Arthur's legendary Knights of the Round Table. See also Percival.

Gorgon: One of 3 hideous sisters in Greek mythology with snakes for hair. They could reputedly turn to stone anyone who met their gaze.

Hall of Cosmic Reflection: A way of describing the Universe/ the Earth, from the viewpoint that everything is a reflection of God. Having created everything, the Divine spark is therefore present in all life.

"Healing Words" blog: http://anitaneilson.com

Kriya: One of the paths of yoga the aim of which is self-realization through the practice of special life-force and meditation techniques.

Maya: The illusion or appearance of the phenomenal world; the veil of delusion through which man believes he is a being of matter and not a being of light.

Medusa: One of the Gorgons. See above.

Moreloveletters.com: See also **sendkidstheworld.com**. A website enabling people to request and receive letters of encouragement from around the world.

Mother Gita: See Bhagavad Gita.

Nicene Creed: The prayer summarizing Christian beliefs, spoken in churches to reaffirm one's faith.

Percival: One of King Arthur's legendary Knights of the Round Table. See also Gawain.

Peter: St. Peter. Christ's apostle who, upon the former's arrest, denied knowing him 3 times.

Prana: The life-force or energy manifest in the Universe.

Saint Teresa of Avila: A 16th century Catholic nun and saint from Avila (Spain) whose iconic writings include the *Interior Castle*.

Samadhi: A high state of meditative consciousness, in which one experiences Oneness with the Universe.

Sandalphon: Archangel Sandalphon reputed to have been the biblical prophet Elijah. Said to be a patron to musicians and is often depicted playing a harp.

Satsang: From Sanskrit "to be in the company of true people", refers to sitting with a Guru or taking part in a group meeting to praise God.

Seasonal Affective Disorder (S.A.D.): A type of winter depression thought to be triggered in some by a reduced exposure to sunlight.

Sendkidstheworld.com: Website devoted to sending postcards to young sick children from around the world. See also **moreloveletters.com**.

Siren: One of the sea nymphs from Greek mythology, part-woman, part-bird, who, by the beauty of their singing, lured sailors to their death on the rocks surrounding their island.

Source: Absolute Creator of all that is. Another name for God or Oneness.

Thrive Global: For "Inner Stillness" Article URL: https://www.thriveglobal.com/stories/10957-inner-stillness-the-joyful-soul-dance

Tug of War: A game where 2 teams hold either end of a rope and try to pull the other team across a central line, in order to claim victory.

Video poems: See YouTube Channel Anita Neilson. Also Healing Words blog Video page: http://anitaneilson.com/video/

Yogi: A practitioner of yoga (meaning "union") philosophy including meditation, selfless action and reforming the self.

BOOKS

O-BOOKS

SPIRITUALITY

O is a symbol of the world, of oneness and unity; this eye
represents knowledge and insight. We publish titles on general
spirituality and living a spiritual life. We aim to inform
and help you on your own journey in this life.
If you have enjoyed this book, why not tell other readers by
posting a review on your preferred book site?
Recent bestsellers from O-Books are:

Heart of Tantric Sex
Diana Richardson
Revealing Eastern secrets of deep love and intimacy
to Western couples.
Paperback: 978-1-90381-637-0 ebook: 978-1-84694-637-0

Crystal Prescriptions
The A-Z guide to over 1,200 symptoms and their healing crystals
Judy Hall
The first in the popular series of six books,
this handy little guide is packed as tight as a pill-bottle
with crystal remedies for ailments.
Paperback: 978-1-90504-740-6 ebook: 978-1-84694-629-5

Take Me To Truth
Undoing the Ego
Nouk Sanchez, Tomas Vieira
The best-selling step-by-step book on shedding the Ego,
using the teachings of *A Course In Miracles*.
Paperback: 978-1-84694-050-7 ebook: 978-1-84694-654-7

The 7 Myths about Love...Actually!
The journey from your HEAD to the HEART of your SOUL
Mike George
Smashes all the myths about LOVE.
Paperback: 978-1-84694-288-4 ebook: 978-1-84694-682-0

The Holy Spirit's Interpretation of the New Testament
A Course in Understanding and Acceptance
Regina Dawn Akers
Following on from the strength of *A Course In Miracles*, NTI
teaches us how to experience the love and oneness of God.
Paperback: 978-1-84694-085-9 ebook: 978-1-78099-083-5

The Message of A Course In Miracles
A translation of the text in plain language
Elizabeth A. Cronkhite
A translation of *A Course in Miracles* into plain,
everyday language for anyone seeking inner peace.
The companion volume, *Practicing A Course In Miracles*,
offers practical lessons and mentoring.
Paperback: 978-1-84694-319-5 ebook: 978-1-84694-642-4

Rising in Love
My Wild and Crazy Ride to Here and Now,
with Amma, the Hugging Saint
Ram Das Batchelder
Rising in Love conveys an author's extraordinary journey
of spiritual awakening with the Guru, Amma.
Paperback: 978-1-78279-687-9 ebook: 978-1-78279-686-2

Thinker's Guide to God
Peter Vardy
An introduction to key issues in the philosophy of religion.
Paperback: 978-1-90381-622-6

Your Simple Path
Find happiness in every step
Ian Tucker
A guide to helping us reconnect with what is really
important in our lives.
Paperback: 978-1-78279-349-6 ebook: 978-1-78279-348-9

365 Days of Wisdom
Daily Messages To Inspire You Through The Year
Dadi Janki
Daily messages which cool the mind, warm the heart
and guide you along your journey.
Paperback: 978-1-84694-863-3 ebook: 978-1-84694-864-0

Body of Wisdom
Women's Spiritual Power and How it Serves
Hilary Hart
Bringing together the dreams and experiences of women across
the world with today's most visionary spiritual teachers.
Paperback: 978-1-78099-696-7 ebook: 978-1-78099-695-0

Dying to Be Free
From Enforced Secrecy to Near Death to True Transformation
Hannah Robinson
After an unexpected accident and near-death experience,
Hannah Robinson found herself radically transforming her life,
while a remarkable new insight altered her relationship
with her father, a practising Catholic priest.
Paperback: 978-1-78535-254-6 ebook: 978-1-78535-255-3

The Ecology of the Soul
A Manual of Peace, Power and Personal Growth
for Real People in the Real World
Aidan Walker
Balance your own inner Ecology of the Soul to regain
your natural state of peace, power and wellbeing.
Paperback: 978-1-78279-850-7 ebook: 978-1-78279-849-1

Not I, Not other than I
The Life and Teachings of Russel Williams
Steve Taylor, Russel Williams
The miraculous life and inspiring teachings of one
of the World's greatest living Sages.
Paperback: 978-1-78279-729-6 ebook: 978-1-78279-728-9

Readers of ebooks can buy or view any of these bestsellers by clicking on the live link in the title. Most titles are published in paperback and as an ebook. Paperbacks are available in traditional bookshops. Both print and ebook formats are available online.

Find more titles and sign up to our readers' newsletter at http://www.johnhuntpublishing.com/mind-body-spirit
Follow us on Facebook at https://www.facebook.com/OBooks/ and Twitter at https://twitter.com/obooks

What people are saying about

Soul Murmurs

These heart-renderings touch deeply, heal and empower even in unsuspecting ways. Let Anita Neilson's brilliant inward light ignite your very own!
Jim Young, Author of *Sip and Savor*

Anita Neilson's compassionates heart is evident as it leaps from the page, as she beckons us all: the ill, the wounded, the lost, and the seeker of Divinity, to take her hand and walk with her on a journey through the seasons. Seasons of the earth, seasons of the heart and emotions, all the circles and cycles of life. Anita Neilson's words are... "like a salve, sealing and protecting" ... as she speaks candidly of her own pain and struggles before venturing to suggest solutions. She gently cautions us, by sharing her life story, that there is more to life than accumulation and material success. The beauty of her homeland leaps from these pages and makes one want to roam the woods and banks of rivers there at any season, to take her book on a long walk through a favorite trail and commune with it under a favorite tree. This elegant collection of seasonal prose and poetry is a balm for the soul; hold her hand and walk through these pages with her and your heart may open to the realm of Divine love, and on the way, you'll take with you some sage advice for living a life in tune with humanity, your own body, and the natural world.
Janavi Held, Poet and Author of *Letters to My Oldest Friend*

Soul Murmurs leads the reader on a beautifully sublime spiritual metamorphosis in tune with the ebb and rhythm of the seasons. Anita's words transfer a calm wisdom that speaks of an inner resilience born of her own transformation. As a former colleague and dear friend, I am delighted to celebrate this treasury of inspirational spiritual poems and prose as wise counsel by your bedside.

Jenny Light, inspirational speaker, yogic meditation teacher, healer and author of *Living Lightly: a journey through Chronic Fatigue Syndrome (M.E.)*, Ayni Books, and *Divine Meditations: 26 Spiritual Qualities of the Bhagavad Gita*, Mantra Books

With a combination of poetry and prose, Anita casts writing spells of Goodness—sowing seeds of compassion and kindness. Her words radiate joy and appreciation for the great dance of impermanence. From cleaning the closets of our mind in Spring, to receiving Winter's invitation as darkness falls to get quiet and still, *Soul Murmurs* offers practical tips, insights, and gorgeous spiritual poems that we can dip into all year long. I am smitten with the joy and ebullience bubbling through on each page. And the poems! Oh the sweet poems—truly they brought me to *That* place. That silent over-flowing abundant silent still fertile joyful place... It reminds me of reading Rilke. I love it.

Mariah McKenzie, Author of *More: Journey to mystical union through the sacred and the profane*, O-Books

Soul
Murmurs

Seasonal words of spiritual
wisdom to enlighten the soul